BORN CRIMINAL

Burning Down the House

Christian Kahner

CBD Productions

"The nature of the criminal justice system has changed. It is no longer primarily concerned with the prevention and punishment of crime, but rather with the management and control of the dispossessed."

MICHELLE ALEXANDER

CONTENTS

PROLOGUE: BORN CRIMINAL

Cesare Lombroso was an 19th century criminologist and psychologist who denied the notion that criminality was a fixture of human nature. Rather, the doctor believed that the penchant for crime was inherited at birth and that this type of unlawful individual could be detected by means of physical, congenital defects. These outward features would confirm that someone was issued into this world as an atavistic throwback to more primitive, "savages," as he deemed them. These biological throwbacks, Lombroso believed, displayed physical characteristics of lower primates, similar to the caricature Neanderthal Man, with protruding foreheads, thick lips, and bone-crushing mandibles. He studied the length of body parts and the circumference of skulls, all in the effort to create a composite sketch of this biological degenerate who would inevitably defy the laws of modern, civilized society. In his studies of these types, Lombroso concluded that these natural outlaws had greater tolerance for pain, keener eyesight, less moral balance, an air of vanity, a pittance of remorse and deep streaks of vindictiveness. They also decorated themselves more frequently with tattoos and shared a common vocabulary among this coterie of thieves. Thus, Lombroso initially concluded that he could identify who would and would not commit crimes through this rubric of physiological representations that were created through the biological lottery of inheritance.

As his life wore on, however, Lombroso was influenced by an

extended family member to believe that social factors could influence an individual and induce, or possibly dissuade, an individual into a life of scoffing at the law. Indeed, Lombroso and his ideas were eventually undermined by a lack of acknowledgement of the prevailing circumstances around the individual. For instances, the lack of remorse for stealing money may have been a pragmatism forged over a lifetime of poverty; in other words, an individual forged a philosophy that lightened the moral weight of stealing when counterbalanced by starvation. One may have a greater tolerance for pain when one has been systematically physically abused his entire life. Tattoos and street slang may have been a necessary social adaptation for survival; just look at the inner-city street gangs of any major city. The 21st century street gang member of the Bloods, Crips, Latin Kings, White Aryan Nation or, in the case of the subject that will be discussed in this book, The Simon City Royals would all seem to be atavistic savages in Lombroso's initial reckoning, as they would easily fit into many of his "scientifically-derived" categories. This categorization, however, would not account for the poverty of inner-cities, or 'hoods, as they are called in the body of this text; it would not acknowledge the lack of a supportive family structure that would assist in creating a positive moral code; it would not accept the desperation of youthful souls on the streets trying to survive hour-to-hour.

Granted, there may be those who are born with built-in predispositions for criminality. The MAOA gene, or The Warrior Gene, is one example of a genetic predisposition that might drive someone towards morally questionable actions because it overloads the system with chemicals that lead to aggressive behavior. On the other hand, similar patterns of behavior can be attained after genetic codes have established at birth. TBI, or Traumatic Brain Injury, has been statistically linked to aggressive behavior, for example. Yet another example is damage to the prefrontal cortex of the brain which can cause "acquired sociopathy," which denotes an acquired, rather than inherited, behavior. If a child were physically abused during childhood by a much larger adult, and this child had been born without any penchant for crime, this individual could develop anti-social behavior patterns due to the violence inherent in the social setting surrounding the otherwise non-criminal human. The combinations are almost endless.

A pupil of Lombroso, Raffaele Garofalo, denied that criminal activity was an act of free will. He did not believe, as our current legal system believes, that criminals are rational actors who are making a calculated decision to commit an act. Garofalo applied the Darwinian concept of adaptation, as in the ability to adapt to society, and the concept of elimination of those who were unable to adapt. While he believed in reparations and partial confinement (for primitive tribes mostly), Lombroso's student did espouse the complete elimination by means of death for those who were incapable through some psychological malady or maladaptation to become a decent member of society. Yes, he championed what supposedly civilized Americans call the Death Penalty, which was the judgment laid upon the protagonist of the tale that follows.

Is taking someone's life justice, however? That is for the reader to decide.The following manuscript is an opportunity to examine this interplay between Nature versus Nurture, Lombroso versus Social Circumstances; it is a chance to see how they intermingle, and in this case, create a human who took a human life and ended up on Death Row, judged by society to be unworthy of life itself, at least initially. Also, it is a chance to examine a personality, which is a complex compound of genetics, surroundings, Fate, chance and random occurrence, as will be apparent in the following tale.

The facts of the case were gathered over the course of dozens of letters that were sent from one of the worst prisons the "civilized" world has to offer, Raiford Correctional Facility in Florida. While the facts of the narrative are true, names have been changed to protect those involved. Yes, these are the very words of a man who did these things, lived this life and has been judged -- rightly or wrongly -- for it all. Now it is time for you, the reader, to be judge and jury and to decide how we become what we are.

BURNING DOWN THE HOUSE: YOUTH

I have to say this much, my feelings on the way he came out of jail the first time changed him. It was like the Devil got him in prison and never let him go. Me [sic] and my dad feel the same way about that. He changed so much for what it's worth. I will always love him no matter what he has done in his life.

DEBRA HILLCREST, ANGEL'S MOTHER

Milwaukee had seen better days before Michael "Angel" Miles started climbing through crawl spaces to break into "side-by-side" houses in working-class neighborhoods, "slinging weed" for chump change and running the streets with the Shorty Folks, the junior division of the 2-1 street gang. Milwaukee had been, during Miles' grandfather's era, a place with a winning baseball team (The Braves led by Hank Aaron and Warren Spahn) and Green Bay lent them a championship football team led by the iconic Vince Lombardi. They were a town of champions who celebrated with beer brewed right down the street in their own neighborhoods; it was a town where a guy could make a living without going off to college. They didn't have to steal, hustle or beg; they just needed to show up Monday morning, without or without the hangover, for work. Someone could support his family by working in any one of the many breweries, factories or mills in the city. It was a strong Midwestern, Middle Class city.

Miles' grandfather worked his whole life as a mechanic for the Coca-Cola Corporation (Miles always mentions proudly), a job that allowed him a house, a family and fishing and hunting trips on the Mississippi River each year.   Whenever the bottom fell out of Miles' mother's life, the hard-working grandfather was there to take her and her children in and to feed them all.

However, by the time Miles' mother was trying to forge the same type of life that had been provided for her by her step-father, things were different. By the final decades of the twentieth century, most of the breweries were gone; industrial jobs were outsourced overseas to save production costs. Unemployment was common. The neighborhoods changed. No one seemed to have any money; everyone was filled with desperation and anxiety. Miles' mother hustled up a semblance of a living working for a vacuum cleaner company, pulling extra shifts to make ends meet. She was gone often. Men came in and out of her life – and the lives of her two boys. They did not know a father figure outside of their grandfather – a case typical of the Post-Industrial cities of the American Midwest. So, Angel like so many of the street kids with whom he ran knew they had to grow up and become men, but they did not have anyone to show them what a grown man was and how a man handled life.

The mood of the town was stressful and dim for many. This anxious, desperate, Post-Industrial working class turned to booze to ease their worried minds, and when that wasn't enough, there were street drugs to provide temporary relief from collections agencies, landlords looking for rent and the hungry kids who filled those rented homes. Families could not bear the stress and, more often than not, they fell apart; divorces were the rule. Kids were raised by foster parents, grandparents, or parents who were working double shifts six days a week – virtually invisible. They were raised by live-in relatives and babysitters who, according to Miles' tale, showed them the streets, drugs, violence, gangsters and ways to get everything they didn't have in life – yet still wanted. These were the shallow substitutes street kids had for steady parents and role models.

So, without supervision, these kids left home and turned to the streets and they banded together. The streets were every bit as mean and distant as the parents who struggled to raise them. Still, groups gathered regionally and formed gangs according to the block they lived on or the neighborhood in which they lived; sometimes gangs formed along racial lines, like the Unknowns and the Latin Kings and the Simon City Royals, the gang that would ultimately claim the loyalty of "Angel" Miles. These kids all brought their damaged beings to the gangs, all with the subtle hope that this new institution would give them the *embrace* they needed, the family structure, the warmth and security for which they yearned. All they had to do to garner these benefits was to be "down for whatever," meaning they had to steal if the gang said to steal, jump a rival, break windows – or even kill – in the name of solidarity.

Miles' mother embodies this struggle between trying to live a decent, if not simple, life in the face of a hostile economy and a desperate society. In a letter, she describes this pattern of the family disintegrating and the child running off into the streets ("out into the world," as she puts it) to make it on his own, by any and all means necessary: "I want to just say that I do not know exactly what it is you want to know. I'm not sure I can write much. You see I myself wasn't around much when my kids were growing up. I worked all the time. I would like to say they had everything in terms of material things. They never did without anything but I was gone a lot. If you would like to call me you can or if you want to make a list of questions I will help you get the answers. This much I can say: my son was never one to lie or tell stories that didn't happen. At one time in our life we were very close like best friends. Then we grew apart. I love my son with all my heart and with all my soul; I would take his place right now if I could. He is and will always be a good boy in my eyes. He always was a follower and not a leader. He was in Lad Lake when he was younger in a "wrap-around" program. He waived himself into the adult courts so he wouldn't go to Wales until he was 18. This is a few things I can tell you …

1. Well, let's start. I wanted him. I know from a real young age I wanted kids, anyway. I had gained like 75 pounds or so carrying him. I was put in the hospital also, because he took a lot out of me. You see I don't drink milk. I haven't from the age – I think – of five because of Head Start School. I got spoiled milk and was sick for a few days because of it. It all tastes spoiled to me. So anyway the hospital is not around anymore. It is an office building or something now. No, my mother and father weren't with me. The guy I fell in love with at 13 was in the waiting room. You see I had a C-section and back then they didn't let dads in for that. My son was not taken out fast enough and ended up getting the crap they give you to put you under. He was rushed to an incubator. It took me a real long time to come to. When the nurse came out in the waiting room to let Michael's dad know he was a boy, she told me later, all the years she was telling men what sex the baby was, she never seen a guy as happy as he was. The sparkle in his eyes, she said she will never forget. We had a nice steak dinner. I of course don't eat steak so Michael's dad got them both. Oh by the way, Michael is a junior. His dad was Michael also. Anyway, I really don't remember much more. I have had the same doctor from when I was older. My grandmother and my mother even saw the doctor. His name was Doctor Yee. He isn't a doctor anymore. He owns a few restaurants. Now from what I remember from back then, I was a young teenager when he was in the middle of buying his first one with all his family. He was a clinical doctor, I think, but we all went to him. He was a good doctor. Oh well, I must say the weather was real hot the year I carried Michael. The month of July was truly hot.

2. Well Michael's dad and I lived together. He lived with us and our younger son, James. He was 26 and was in Denver prison for almost three years. He came home right when they released him to me. They "exposed" him here. I have been in love with Michael's dad pretty much near my whole

life. I met him when I was 13. He was 15 almost 16 and Michael looks very much like him. His dad is almost 51 in March. No he really wasn't much a part of the boy's life. We went our own ways when Michael was a few months old. Michael got married to a girl he got pregnant while he was with me. He left me and that was the end of the first part of our life together. I can tell you this much: he is very bi-polar and it gets very difficult some days to deal with him, but I truly love him and I have for just about ever. I was married to a man when Michael was just about 7. I stayed married to him until I left him when my son James was just about 17. Then I got back with Michael's and James' dad and tried again. For about how long, I don't know how long, this time it lasted. You see, all these years were on and off for so many years me and Michael [sr.] would be together. So many times back and forth. We don't even always get along, I can say with my heart, I truly am in love with him and always will be, no matter what happens from now until the end of time that will, for sure, never change. You see that's the only thing I can be 100% sure about in my life.

3.   My dad was a big part of Michael's life. I lived at home back and forth many times. My parents took care of Michael and James a lot. I remember one time when I was living at home, the boys were pretty little, me and my dad got into a big fight about something – can't really remember what it was even about. But he told me to get out of his house and, mind you, it was night time. He wanted me to get out but he wouldn't let me take my boys with me. I had to call the police. They came out and it was raining this night. The police told me he couldn't keep my children. The officer talked me into leaving my children with them. For the night, my dad told them we could stay. So that was that, it's just one night I won't ever forget. My dad, I mean the man who helped my mother bring me into this world, is dead. The only man I know as my Dad is my dad [Angel's grandfather]. I was three years old when my mother got with my dad. My dad was all

about doing for his family. He made sure we had everything. That is something he instilled on me for sure because I was just like that with my boys. My real dad is in my life; my biological dad beat my mother even when she was carrying one of us, pretty bad. He was shot down by the police because he escaped from jail and he, I guess, drew a gun. It was so long ago, but I do remember once right before that all took place, my grandmother took me to see him in prison. I can't tell you what prison, but I do remember a long hallway with wood benches along the walls and my grandma sat down and my dad was right there. He picked me up and sat me down on his knee and I remember the vending machines right next to us. My dad bought me a candy bar. I do remember this as if it was just from an hour ago on this day. Anyway, and to go on, I think my dad was in the army but was discharged. That was before my time, so to go on, my dad has changed a lot from when I was a kid growing up. I would need a few months to get into all that. So I will just say this, he did a lot for his kids, me and my brother. He died a few years back, about 5 years ago, and he did a lot for his grandsons and he still is doing for me and he is retired for 3 years now. Michael doesn't talk about his grandmother because she died when he was in prison the first time.

4.   I lost everything I owned twice. Once to a fire and once to a time in my life when all my things went into storage and I had no way to pay the bill and lost it all. So I don't have anything from the past. I have some pictures but that is it. I truly can't recall the school thing. They went to a few different schools when he even went. I know he skipped a lot, partied with his friends a lot. You see, I didn't know much until way after these years went by about a lot of the stuff he did or was doing. He broke into a house by us. It was two homes down from us. His friend lived there. I'm not sure the stuff that he took. I'm not sure what took place after that. My Michael was always the follower. Never the leader.

5.   I don't remember when he really started acting out. He left

home at like 15. He was staying with, at the time, an older girlfriend and her mother and sister. He went to Lad Lake this time because I remember taking her out to see him when we went. Anyway he was away from home more than I can say.

6.   My best memory was the day I had him. I wanted him. He really was my life, at least back then I felt like that. Me and Michael were able to talk like best friends about everything. We even smoked pot together and that is something I stopped doing a long time ago. We got together when he came over to the house. He was already grown and out in the world. I have to say this much, my feelings on the way he came out of jail the first time changed him. It was like the Devil got him in prison and never let him go. Me and my dad feel the same way about that. He changed so much for what it's worth. I will always love him no matter what he has done in his life.

Miles and his mother would remain close through all of his trips to diversion programs, boot camps, jails and ultimately prison. Though she swore it was prison that put the Devil in him, she dubbed him "Angel" when she went to visit him at Jacksonville Correctional Institution. It may be the rose-colored glasses of a mother trying to remember the better parts of her son's life, or there may even be a strain of guilt tainting her memories, but, either way, according to Miles himself, his life reads like a catalog of mishaps, brutal accidents, failures, and impulsive decisions – all dashed with moments of lust and intoxication.

Miles' birth itself was a near-disaster that landed him in an incubator and the life that followed seemed to be filled with the same. Worse than the disaster and the turbulence that seemed to haunt him was the fact there was a void around him and a suspicious emptiness inside of him. He always wanted things that were not his, that he could not have and that no one seemed to have the time or money to give him – everyone was broke and hustling. Miley sensed his life was as desperate as the failing city around him – and it all started early on. Constantly, even maniacally, he was stealing life. In a jailhouse poem, Miley raps about his early despair:

> *They wanna know,*
> *What the fuck I was thinking when I was out there on the block*
> *When I drove to Florida and killed a fuckin' cop?*
> *To live a life full of sin*
> *When I was facing life in the pen.*
> *What the fuck I was thinkin'?*
> *What the fuck I was thinkin'?*
> *They wanna know*
> *So now … here I am trying to tell them as best I can,*
> *At age 8 is when my life began … getting out of hand …*
> *I was out there on the streets with nothing to do …*

Filled with such angst so early on, Miles took his first steps towards that six-by-nine cell on Death Row hundreds of miles away from his hometown of Milwaukee, doomed to death for killing a "cop." It was approximately two years earlier, at the age of six, that Miles almost ended his own life – as well as the lives of his beloved mother and younger brother, James. Miles does not remember childhood memories of playing in the park with his father as a toddler, his first birthdays parties, the first days of school or his best friends from that time; no, his recollections of life seem to begin with the day that he destroyed his family's home and what little they had; he remembers how he hospitalized his family for a full year. Thus, his memory is wrapped in a fog of physical damage and the ravages of alcohol and drug abuse. In fact, during his capital murder trial his brain was likened to that of a senior citizen with dementia, one who could barely perceive reality.

In spite of the early trauma in his life and his faulty memory, Miles still feels the need to explain precisely how he ended up a condemned man, starting with his earliest memories:

"In my mind my life is filled with many different chapters. The furthest back I can recall is where I was about six. I'll get to that in a moment. I was born and raised in Milwaukee, Wisconsin. My mother Deborah had me in 1982 when she was 20 or 21. My father's name is Michael and I'm a junior. My parents were alcoholics and I believe my father was using cocaine and crack. From what I was told, my dad bounced in and out of our lives for a few years after I was born. My mother had another son born in '84, named James. My earliest memory is of when I was around six. My father was no longer around. My mother, brother and I lived on the East Side of Milwaukee in an upstairs duplex with a black lab dog as a family pet.

"I don't recall anything from that time.

"I only remember one incident which changed all of our lives. Mom worked long hours at a Kirby vacuum company. When she was home, she often slept, which meant James and I had the run of the house. One of these days that she was asleep, I snuck in her room and stole her lighter. James and I went to our bedroom to play with it. I didn't like the cartoon characters on my sheets that were on my bed. James and I had a bunk bed. I thought it would be a good idea to set the sheet on fire. Next thing we knew, the whole bunk bed was ablaze and we couldn't put it out. Next thing I remember is firemen fighting to put the flames out and telling us to get out of the house. Today I don't know what exactly happened. The whole house burned up. I vaguely recall trying to open a door to get out and the doorknob burning my hand. Then I got out by jumping out of the second floor window. When the fire department got there, they found my mom lying unconscious in our bedroom. They found my brother unconscious in the kitchen. Our dog was lying on top of his body protecting him partially from the flames. My mom received burns over 75% of her body. James was almost in as bad of a shape as her. Both almost died and spent over a year hospitalized. James had to go through speech and physical therapy for a year .He literally had to learn how to walk, talk, eat, etc. all over again like a baby would.

"During the time they were in the hospital I lived with my grandparents, Herbert and Patricia. They were my mom's parents. At the hospital, I was scared to death. I was scared because I didn't want to see how bad she was hurt 'cause of me. A little kid that age has all kinds of crazy, irrational fear. I was surprised by my mom's reaction when I did see her. With the burns on her face and body, the hugs and kisses caused her a great amount of pain. She would spend our visit trying to comfort me and assure me that I wasn't to blame for what happened. I didn't like visiting them at the hospital, 'cause what I did to them caused such a deep sorrow, which I could never excuse myself for. Even after all the skin graft, 20 years later, they still have burn scars on their faces and bodies. James has learning disabilities and is borderline retarded. We lost everything we owned in that fire. My grandparents took my mom and brother into their home when they were released from the hospital, only a mile away from the home I burned down.

"Being with my grandparents was pretty cool. James and I went to a school which was only one block from our house. Times are a blur for me. It was the most stable and healthy environment I ever lived in, though. My grandpa had a good job working as a mechanic for Coca Cola. For James and me it was like he was a superhero and could never do any wrong. Grandpa spent a lot of time with us after work and on weekends. He would take us everywhere with him. Weekends, we would go to museums. He took us to the library often to check out books and teach us new things. We went to parks to play catch with the football, basketball, baseball, soccer, Frisbee or to just hang out. During the winter, he often took us to places to go sledding. During the summer, he loved taking us fishing. We always had a lot of fun. Grandma would come with us on some of these occasions. We loved her but didn't like her because she was the one to always tell us how we were to be punished. That was only because grandpa never denied us anything we wanted and never really punished us for anything. He believed in talking to us when we did wrong in trying to teach us. Grandma believed we needed consequences for our bad actions. We never got physical punishment such as spanked or hit by either of them. Grandma would just ground us to the house or she would take privileges away. They were both the best grandparents a kid could ask for, though. Grandma always had dinner on the table ready for us when grandpa got home from work. We always ate together at the table as a family. On weekends, grandma always made us huge breakfasts. Sausage links, sausage patties, bacon, hash browns, egg omelet's with ham, onion, cheese, green peppers, yolk eggs, scrambled eggs, toast, French toast, orange juice, apple juice, and more. She loved to cook for us and we love to eat her food. After meals, James and I would sit on grandpa's lap and he would read stuff to us from the newspaper. We had to do chores every day like sweeping, dishes, vacuuming, dusting. I had only one friend named Joey at that time. He went to the same school and lived only three blocks from us. I spent a lot of time with him. Mostly we played in the park.

"Somewhere in that time, Mom got married to my step-dad named, Brad. I'll get to that chapter in a minute. First, I want to tell you about some of the stupid things I did as a little kid. As I said, my grandpa is a mechanic. He worked on car engines in our garage during his free time. James and I love to hang around in the garage and watch him and play with his tools. One time he was under a car working on it and I found a jar of used car oil. For whatever reason, I decided to drink it. It wasn't a very smart thing to do. Grandpa had to rush me to the hospital and I had to drink this charcoal liquid to clean out my system. Another time the whole family was going to a family friend's house for a barbecue and swim in their 8- foot -deep pool. When we arrived in front of the house, I jumped out of the car and ran to the backyard by the pool. I climbed onto the pool deck and jumped right into the pool. I'd always loved water, but unfortunately at that time I hadn't learned how to swim yet. Lucky for me, my family heard the splash of me jumping in the pool while they were headed to the back yard. My grandpa jumped in to the pool, climbed the deck, and dove in after me. He pulled me out and started CPR. When I spit out the water and opened my eyes, I started laughing. I guess I thought it was funny. Grandpa was still wearing all his clothes, and had his watch on and wallet in his pocket. I didn't even understand I could have died.

"Okay, so mom got married to Brad and we moved into our own house on 20th and Scott on the Southside. This is where my life started taking a huge turn. For those not familiar with Milwaukee, this neighborhood is infested with gangs, drugs, violence and crime. A typical 'hood[1] of poverty. We had a lot of family that lived in this 'hood. My aunt Barb

and her husband Carol lived on 20th and Scott. They had like nine children that were all grown. Aunt Barb had several kids by another man before Carol. I only know of my cousins Mary Jane, John, Wayne and Howard. They were my white cousins. Carol was black so their kids, Junior and Mike, were mixed. John, Mike, Carol and Aunt Barb all live together. My Cousin Mary Jane lived in a house right next door to them. At that time, she had my cousin Howard and two kids living there. Her kids were my cousins, Latoya and Shawn. They are both mixed. Toya is my age and Shawn is two years younger. Soon after came Mary's son, Shane, who is mixed. My cousin Mike is about seven years older than me.

"Mom was still working at a Kirby 'cause the owner, Pauline, was also her close friend. Pauline gave mom her job back after she recovered from the fire. Mom seemed to work overtime all the time and was hardly ever home. I think she worked so much to try and replace all the stuff we lost in the fire and still be able to provide for us. Brad worked at some factory and painted houses on the side whenever he could find that work. James and I never liked him or got along with him. Brad was an alcoholic and abused us both on a daily basis -- both mentally and physically. Mom was aware of some of it but not all of it. I spent a lot of my time at my cousin's house. Toya, Shawn, James, and I were always together.   Brad was racist and would say stupid, racial comments to my cousins when they were around, so we didn't like hanging at my house. We ran the streets with other kids from the 'hood. First two kids I met and got close to were Juanito and his little brother Lito. Juanito is a year older than me and Lito two years younger. They are half Puerto Rican

and half Mexican .He also lived on 20th and Scott. Their mother's name is Carmen and she was a single mom with two other daughters named Heidi and Seinee. Both were very young. Later came another son named Winter.

"Juanito, Lito and I were best friends for a long time. First we spent a lot of time doing what I consider normal stuff for kids our age. We were about eight or nine when we met. When we met, we loved going to a park called Mitchell Park about 10 blocks from our house. It had a pond where we could catch frogs, turtles, tadpoles, and fish. We would wade in the mucky seaweed water and catch stuff with the net. There were these trees close by the water that had vine-like branches which we would grab a hold of and swing into the pond. During the winter, we liked to play on the ice or sled on the hills. We roamed the 'hood and discovered a lot of yards that had apple trees, grape vines, pear trees, or gardens with vegetables. We loved to steal from them and eat the stuff.

"We had a thing for climbing onto the tops of garages and buildings. That's where we would eat our fruits, vegetables and talk. Before long, we met a girl named Melissa who moved into the house next to Juanito. She was our age and had two younger brothers. They were all Latino. I started having interests in girls and Juanito and I we're both trying to get Melissa as our girlfriend. Juanito, Toya and I used to always hang together 'cause we're all about the same age. A lot of times we had Shawn, James and Lito with us because they were our little brothers and always wanted to be with us. Juanito and I started experimenting sexually with Melissa and Toya. I knew it was wrong because I was too young, but I didn't understand that it wasn't right to do those things with family. I never had intercourse with either of them. We would get naked and touch each other. Juanito had sex with them both. We usually did this stuff at one of our houses in either an attic or the basement. I could have had sex with them both, but I was scared and didn't know what I was doing.

"Around that time, my cousin Wayne moved into my house and lived in our attic. He was in his thirties and watched James and me when our parents weren't home. One night he came into my room where I was supposed to be sleeping. I pretended to be a sleep, so I wouldn't get into trouble. He came to my bed and removed my blanket. I kept my eyes shut. Then he slid his hand down my underwear and began fondling my penis. I was so scared I just kept my eyes closed and prayed he would leave. After a few minutes of this, I stirred and faked like I was waking up. Then he hurried up and left my room. I was scared to go to sleep for months after that. He did it again a few weeks later. This time I really was sleeping. I woke up and asked him why he was touching me. I was mad when he said he wasn't. I told him I would tell my mom if he ever did it again. I thought I would be in trouble if I told .I never did tell a soul about that until recently. I felt ashamed, and felt it was my fault for some reason. Even now, I still feel ashamed and was hesitant write about it. Only reason I am is because I want you, the reader, to know the whole truth about my life and the events that took place to get me where I am today … Death Row.

"Wayne moved out shortly after and my older cousin, Haley, moved in and became our baby sitter. Both my parents were working a lot and we needed someone to watch us. That's when I was introduced to the gangs, crime, drugs, sex, violence and much more. Haley is about 10 years older than I am. My 'hood was infested with local gangs. There are the 2-1's, known as the 21st Street Gangsters. That's the older crew for like 16 and up to the late thirties. Then there is the SF, known as "Shorty folks." They are a gang for kids under 16 and that gang is under the 2-1's. In the surrounding area there are two other gangs called the Unknowns and Latin Kings. They are rival gangs.

"About the time Haley moved in I started hanging with my cousin Mike. He was a member of the 2-1 gang. He started teaching me how to steal from stores. I remember one time I learned I could stick my arm inside cigarette machines and steal all the packs of cigarettes 'cause my arm was long and thin. I used to go to this George Webb's Restaurant that had cigarette machines in the lobby. Mike would be my look-out and I would literally steal every pack of cigarettes out of the machine. Afterwards, we would go to the bars and Mike would sell the packs of cigarettes at a discount while I would wait outside.

"We did this one day and didn't sell all the packs. I had started smoking. That night, I went home with about 30 packs or so on me and smelling like smoke. Mom smelled some of the smoke on me as soon as I walked in the door. She searched me and found all the packs I had and all the money I had 'cause of the packs we had sold. Boy, was she mad. I had a choice to tell her where I got the stuff or get whooped. I told her everything. She took a Polaroid photo of me and then took me to the restaurant. She told the manager what I did, gave him the cigarettes and money, gave him a photo of me with our phone number, and told him to call the police and then her if they ever seen me in there again.

"Later that night as punishment for smoking, my parents made me smoke five cigars. I guess they thought it would make me really sick and make me not want to smoke again. I acted like I hated it but, really, I didn't. After the second cigar, I will say I began to feel sick. I did get grounded to the house also, but that didn't stick because my parents weren't ever home to enforce it. After that incident I started stealing from Walgreens and getting cigars to smoke for me and my friends.

"Haley's boyfriend was the leader of the 2-1's at that time. He lived on 20th and Scott. Every day when my parents were at a work, she would have him over to our house. With him came several of his gang buddies. They would drink and smoke weed while Haley and Dennis were in the bedroom having sex. James and I would listen to them telling stories and planning crimes. They would tell us to drink from their liquor and smoke their weed. Mostly just me, though, 'cause of the fact James was too young. I wanted to be cool like them and for them to like me, so I did it. Haley was a cool adult but she wasn't OK with us doing those things, so we heard it from her. After a while though, they would do it in front of her and if she protested they would tell her to stop trippin'[2]. So, eventually, she just accepted it.

"I don't remember why but Haley ended up moving out

and moving in with my Cousin Mary on 20th. Although Mary was in her thirties and had three kids, she was a party person. Her daughter Toya pretty much took care of her brothers, Shawn and Shane, even though she was just a kid herself. When Haley moved in Toya didn't have to do as much. I hung out and spent the night at my cousin's as much as I could. There were always gang parties there and anyone could crash overnight. Juanito often spent the night there, too. The 2-1's used to beat on us all the time and say it was to toughen us up. In turn, Toya, Juanito, and I would beat on our little brothers thinking we were making them tough. The house was always a mess with liquor bottles everywhere, trash everywhere, dishes everywhere, and roaches everywhere. There was never much to eat, if anything at all.

"I remember on several occasions the 2-1's sent Juanito, Toya, Shawn, James and me to do dirty work for them. An Unknown lived three houses down from Mary's house. They had us throw bricks through his front bay window a few different times. Some Latin Kings moved in a place at the end of the block. We were ordered to bust out every window in their house. It was either do it or get beaten for being pussy. Between my step-dad beating on me all the time when he was drunk , mom spanking me all the time with belts for being bad, and the 2-1's beating on me just because, I started to think it was normal, though the same stuff was happening to my friends and cousins.

"A girl my age named Haley moved into a house directly across the street from Juanito. She had a brother named Jerry who was about seven years older. Her parents were Lester and Laurie. They were Foster Care parents to other kids as well. Juanito and I started to spend more time and nights at his house since there was Melissa next door and Haley across the street. His mom, Carmen, didn't mind 'cause she liked me. She was also out partying most of the time anyway, and I had got so good at stealing that she used to take me to malls just to steal her a bunch of expensive clothes. One time, she offered to give me a pager that was hooked up for life and you didn't have to pay any bills. That was huge to me back then. I stole her what she wanted and she gave me the pager. Anyway, when we met Haley, I wanted to be around her all the time .We liked each other but I was too shy to ask her to be my girl. Juanito ended up dating her, but that didn't last long.

"Haley and I started dating. Something happened where Carmen got her kids taken from her and Haley's parents took in Juanito, Lito, Heidi and Winter as foster kids. At that time, I thought that was pretty cool 'cause it meant I got to spend a lot of time with Haley and her parents would think I was there were for Juanito and Lito. I even spent the night often. At night, I would sneak into Haley's room and we would fool around for a while when everyone was asleep. Mostly we just did a lot of kissing and touching each other. I loved sucking on her tits and just laying my head on them 'cause they were so soft and big. She was my first girlfriend and first love. We had planned to have sex on my birthday for the first time. I was turning either 11 or 12. My parents were letting me have a sleepover party for close friends, and we were all going to spend the night in my attic. Juanito and I ended up getting into some kind of trouble together before the party and my parents canceled it. I think that was the time the 2-1's sent us to steal for them and we got caught. They were always having us doing shit we had no business doing. We just wanted to fit in.

"Juanito and I decided to join the Shorty Folks. To join, I had to stand in a circle with six of them around me and take the 3 minutes of beating by them -- all at the same time. I took my ass whooping first. I have a high tolerance for pain because of the physical abuse from my step dad and the 2-1's. I didn't enjoy the beating, but it didn't bother me. Juanito started to get jumped in after me, but after 30 seconds of being beat down, he couldn't take it no more and called it off. He was crying and I really felt bad for my friend, but I was also embarrassed. The Shorty Folk saw him as a pussy after that and no longer had respect for him .I was given the nickname Blades and I started spray painting it on garages and houses et cetera. I always took risks that most people wouldn't. I would go into rival territory a lot and spray-paint SF art on the Latin Kings' work. I was chased off a lot and even shot at a few times for doing this. None of that mattered to me, though. I wanted my cousins and the 2-1's to be impressed with me, to show me love and respect. Those were the people I looked up to and thought were cool.

"I remember one time some Unknowns did a drive by, shooting up my cousin's house. A 2-1 ended up shooting back at the car and hitting an Unknown with a bullet in the head. The 2-1 didn't die, but he wasn't the same after that. And the 2-1's had beef with the Kings and about forty 2-1's, including my cousin Haley, met up at a school playground across the street from my house. They were passing around guns and planning an attack on the Kings. A brown Cadillac rolled by and several guns opened fire on us. Most of us dropped to the ground to avoid being hit but one guy still caught a bullet in his forearm .When the police and ambulances arrived, it was chaos. I heard police saying things to each other like "I wish they would have killed each other, "too bad only one got shot," and crap like that.

"After that, the cops started harassing any 2-1 they saw. To get even for it, some 2-1's jumped a cop, beating him real good and stealing his police belt. They got his gun that time, cuffs and the whole works. I was taking the view that the police was just another rival gang; that this was a gang that could kill you and get away with it every time. Knowing this made me avoid them as much as possible. I was only 10 or 11.

"I went home to find my step-dad drunk. He started getting loud with me and asking if I was out running the streets and getting into trouble with those no good cousins. Usually, I just ignored his stupid, racist remarks but I didn't that day. I told him to go fuck himself .He got in my face yelling and poking me with his finger. I was so mad I punched him in his face. He ended up beating the crap out of me. That was the first time I ever hit him or tried to fight back. I had a black eye, a busted lip, and plenty of bruises. For some reason, I thought my mom was going to be mad at me, so I ran away from home before she came home from work. I knew they called the police and everyone was looking for me so I stayed away from all the people I usually hung around.

"I had a friend named Preston who used to live on 20[th,] but had moved to Sixth and National. He was a mixed kid my age and lived with his mom and two older brothers; Johnny and Adam. I didn't hang with him much once he moved 'cause where he moved was a King 'hood. My family didn't know where he lived. I stayed with them for several weeks. That was a wild time for me. We had to do anything we could to provide for ourselves. Most days were spent going from store to store and stealing. We stole food to eat, clothes to wear, cigarettes, alcohol, anything we could. Whatever we didn't keep for our own use, we would sell on the streets. We broke into a lot of vehicles to steal CD's and whatever we could find.

"I don't remember how I eventually got back home. When I was 12, we moved to a suburban neighborhood inside a side-by

side house right off a 107th Street and Brown Deer Road. It was a very good area. Didn't live there very long. I started hanging with a group of kids that were a little older than me. They were fairly good kids compared to the bunch I was used to hanging with. Their idea of a good time was hanging out in the garage drinking and smoking weed. We did that often. There was a gated fenced-in community pool we used to go to a lot in the middle of the night. We would jump the fences and skinny dip in the pool. We had some good times.

"Then a guy in his younger twenties moved in a few houses from me. I started hanging with him and he convinced me to break into his neighbor's house. Then, into my neighbor's. We both lived in side-by -side houses and we had adjoining attics where each side had a crawl space. I crawled through my side of the house and entered the neighbor's house through their crawl space. The guy had told me to steal any money, jewelry, any things that looked expensive. He gave me a few dollars. Later that day, the police showed up at his house and mine. That dude got caught with stolen stuff and snitched on me. He went to jail because of his age but the neighbor didn't want to press charges on me.

"Unfortunately, around the same time, I got in trouble for stealing a hammer from a construction site and my little brother James was accused of trying to molest a younger neighbor. We got evicted after all that. I believe we ended up staying with my cousin Mary Jane for a few months before we got our own house on 84th and Green Tree Road. The time frame of events until that time is all kind of blurred together in my mind. I was constantly bouncing around living with my grandparents, cousins or mom and step dad, all those years. I don't remember much of my years in elementary school. I started off well, but after the fire I ended up getting bounced around for a while. In schools, I had a problem adjusting to classmates and teachers. Mom finally got me back into this one school after several failed attempts at other schools. James went there too because they had the Special Ed. Classes he needed.

"At school I was always the class clown and center of attention. When I lived with my grandparents I went to school every day, but was often late even though the school was only one block away. I didn't like waking up early and a lot of times would be late because I lost track of time watching cartoons.

"When I lived with my parents, I had to take a school bus. I was a pretty good student until up to fifth grade. I guess it was the hanging with my cousin Haley and her 2-1 friends that started taking an effect on me. In fifth grade, we had a field trip to go to the zoo. We had to turn in like $12.00 each to our teacher for the trip. But I knew our teacher put everyone's field trip money inside a locked file cabinet .A few days before the trip, I broke into the file cabinet and stole the money. I never got caught and the school had to pay for everyone's field trip. We went to the zoo. There was one of the concession stands that nobody worked at yet, so I went behind it and stole boxes of candy and filled my book bag up. When we got back to school, I started selling boxes of candy to the kids. Someone snitched on me. I got suspended and my parents had to pay the zoo back for what I stole.

"We used to be able to do a book reports for extra credit and get certificates for free pizzas from the teacher. Every week I would go into the teacher's desk and steal 10 certificates so my friend Joey and I could get free pizza from a Little Caesars every day after school .We would forge the teacher's signature on them and never got caught.

"This school had classes for first through eighth grade. I went to school there until the middle of seventh grade. I often got suspended for one reason or another. Most of the time, it was for selling stuff. I'd steal boxes of candy and candy bars from stores and sell the stock at school. When I had to take the bus to school, I skipped school a lot. I'd tell mom I missed the school bus so I could stay home. At first, she started taking me to school herself before work if I missed the bus, but that always made her late to work. It wasn't that I didn't like school either. I just wanted to hang with my cousin Haley and the 2-1's all the time. I felt like I was going to miss something if I was at school.

"When we moved to 84th street, I transferred to a school two blocks away from our house right in the middle of seventh grade. There weren't many white kids that went there. I got close to a few kids there, namely a kid named Brad that was my age and a lot like me. I found out he lived about 2 miles from my house so we became good friends out of school too. We skipped classes a lot to hang in the school halls and smoke weed.

"My parents worked between 8:00 am and 4:00 pm so I was able to skip and just chill at home, too. Those were times when Brad and I would skip with a few friends just to hang in my house, listen to music, drink, and get high. That ended after some of our so-called friends robbed my house. I left the door unlocked so we could meet at my house. When Brad and I got there, they had already been there and left. They stole a bunch of stuff, but nothing major. I had to tell my mom what happened. After that, I only trusted Brad and stopped hanging with the others. There was a day that was called "Kill Whitey Day" where black kids would beat up any white kid. Most of the white kids stayed home, but not Brad and I. Turned out to be a crazy day for us. We got in a whole lot of fighting and running. Eventually, we were cornered in the hall and the principal got called in. We got suspended and they called Brad's mom to pick him up.

"When she got there, she was drunk. The principal told her what happened and she went off on the principal and every school administrator that could hear. Before we knew what was happening, she had dragged Brad and I both out of the school to her car. She wasn't mad at us at all and we spent the rest of that day chilling at his house.

"After that happened, we started skipping a lot more. My neighborhood didn't have any kids my age. They were kids that were getting ready to graduate from high school and go to college. That didn't stop me from hanging with them though. I grew up hanging with the older crowd, so I fit in pretty good. This group of kids wasn't about gangs or getting into any trouble. They spent most of their free time playing basketball or cruising the strip looking for girls. I was pretty good at ball so I played with them often. We had a basketball hoop connected to our garage, so they played there are a lot. Plus we had a pool table in our basement and they liked to play. For years as a little kid my mom used to take me to bars with her all the time. I didn't have much else to do but play pool and shoot darts, so I got really good at all over the years. The older kids and even adults liked playing me.

"My step-dad's family used to have get-togethers for the holidays and I've met some of my cousins during that time .The one cousin I related to the most was Paul. He was my age and we started hanging out a lot, and we would get into all kinds of trouble. We love to wait until everyone was asleep and then get dressed up in military gear and go on missions. Looking back at it now, it was some real silly stuff we did. We would dress in all black, wearing ski masks and gloves and have belts with our tools on it like flash lights, screwdrivers etc.. We would carry backpacks. We would sneak out and break into vehicles and garages to steal.

"Paul ended up introducing me to a girl named Carrie that actually lived not far from my house. The first time there, a girl named Heather had stopped by. When she came into the house, she was giving everyone hugs. As I laid eyes on her, I was in awe. She was fifteen, 5 feet tall, had long curly black hair, 100 pounds, beautiful chocolate brown eyes, and big breasts. Something just came over to me, and I knew right then I wanted her to be my girl. Before anyone had a chance, I introduced myself to her and said I'd like a hug -- everyone else had gotten one. She smiled and gave me a hug. I held her a little longer than I should have, but I could tell she was feeling[3] me.

"We all hung out for a few hours and I found out Heather had a boyfriend she recently started seeing named Todd. He made me step up my game to show her I'd be better for her. When I was ready to go I asked Heather if she would walk with me to the corner and she did. We did a lot of flirting at first and when we got to the corner, I asked for a hug. She gave me a hug and this time she was the one who didn't want to let go. After the hug, I gave her my number and held her again. I asked if I could kiss her and she said she had a man. A bus was coming so I jokingly told her if she wouldn't kiss me, I'd jump in front of it.

She laughed at me and pulled me to her and gave me a passionate kiss that had my whole body feeling like putty. That was the start of what has now been a 15-year relationship/friendship.

"At that point, I started to really get interested in girls. Heather and I hooked up .We spent a lot of our time together hanging out at Carrie's house. Heather had a sister named Rachel that was a year younger than Carrie; Rachel was nothing like Heather, though. She was a lot more shy and reserved. Rachel was a beautiful girl, with long blond hair, blue eyes, 5'9", 110 pounds, and perky breasts. Carrie looked similar to her except she had brown eyes, was a little taller, and was flat-chested. I started bringing Brad with me when I went to Carrie's. A lot of the time he would be alone and he could hook up with one of the girls. He did eventually hook up with Rachel.

"All of us would go to stores and Brad and I would steal things to get for the girls. None of them ever asked us. We just enjoyed those smiles on their faces. Usually, it was only makeup, perfumes, gold and stuff like that. My mom really like Heather and was used to having people stay over at night. Heather spent Easter with me and my family so she stayed all night that day before. 'Course, mom said one of us could sleep in my bed and the other had to sleep on the floor. We ended up in bed together and made love for our first time. I was nervous and a little clumsy but the experience was wonderful. I must not have done too bad 'cause she didn't believe that was the first time I ever had sex. Till this day, she doesn't believe it. Heather spent part of Easter day with my family; then she left, saying she needed to spend time with her own family. Later, I found out she actually went to spend time with Todd, his family, and even stayed the night. But I never let it show. I didn't even tell her I knew about it.

"I was over at Carries house and Carrie pulled me aside saying she really needed to talk me. I went with Carrie to another room where Rachel was alone and crying. She told me she didn't want to be with Brad and broke up with him. I was shocked when she pulled me to her and kissed me. She knew I was with her sister but didn't care. She said we could be together and

Heather didn't have to know. As I hadn't forgotten what Heather did to me, I agreed with no hesitation. Plus, she was extremely attractive and her lips were so soft I wanted to kiss her forever if I could. This secret went on for a few days. Then one day Carrie asked me to help her with something in the backyard. I get back there and she told me to sit down on a lawn chair. Before I knew what was going on, she straddled herself on my lap facing me. I played it off cool and told her I knew that she wanted me. We started kissing and feeling each other up. She told me she wanted to fool around from time to time but Heather or Rachel couldn't find out. I couldn't believe my luck.

"That same night I went home and called Heather. It just so happened that Rachel asked to speak to me and Heather let her. As soon as she got on the phone, the tears started and the speech followed. She told me and she couldn't continue the relationship with me and do that to her sister. Before I could even respond, Heather was back on the phone breaking up with me too. The phone line went dead and I sat there for a minute to try to understand what the hell had just happened here. I let some hours pass before I called back so she could cool down. When we spoke again I broke everything down to her about knowing how she played me and going to Todd's house, how I was feeling hurt, and how I was sorry about that mistake I made. We agreed to forgive each other and stay together. Her parents had recently split up and her dad was living with his girlfriend. I was there to comfort her through that painful ordeal. The first night I spent at her house, we made love all night long listening to slow love songs and had the room lit up with a red light. It was a great night. We stayed the night at each other's houses as often as possible, but for the most part, she was always at my house. When my parents were not at home, we were like jack rabbits, screwing each other's brains out up to a dozen times a day. We fucked on the bed, floors, chairs, pool table, bar stools, kitchen table, sink, toilet, washer and dryer, or, against a wall, or inside the shower. Every place you could imagine -- we didn't care. Sex being new to both of us, them were our experimental days. It went on like that for a year every day and it was great.

"For my whole life, my grandparents have always taken my parents and us kids on vacation with them every summer. There we would fish on the Mississippi River. They would lease a cottage from a friend that was overlooking the river. Heather started coming to these family vacations with us; she came to not only these, but every other event as well. Grandfather took me to a course and I got my hunting licenses, so I could go deer hunting with him and his buddies. She came along for that as well. At first, his buddies were a little off, having a young girl staying in same hotel room with us, but they all really liked her and it didn't take long for them to get comfortable. I though Heather would do a lot of complaining about being in the cold, outside all day and trudging through the woods. Surprisingly, she was a trooper and we had fun.

"During that trip, I stole a bottle of schnapps from the hotel bar for us to drink. My grandfather, step dad, and his buddies always took us to the bar with them during hunting trips. We would spend that time shooting pool, playing darts, or gambling on arcade video poker game. Later in the hotel we would all play poker for change. I won a little money and bought Heather a glass rose that said *I Love You* from the gift shop.

"Our times spent on the Mississippi River together weren't as much fun. She really didn't care much for fishing and didn't know how to swim. I, on the other hand, loved doing both. I tried teaching her how to swim but she was scared of the water. She was wearing a life jacket and I dragged her ass out into deep water and she kicked and screamed the whole time. After that, she wouldn't even get into the water again. One time my parents took us to a campground called Plymouth Rock. They had just bought a new car and given me their Sunbird. I didn't have my license but Heather did, so we followed them to the campground. We had a great time playing bingo at the bingo hall, roasting marshmallows around the fire, and just hanging out. My parents and little brother James all stayed in one big tent. Heather and I had our own small tent.

"There was a night where everyone went to sleep and we decided we wanted to make love outside the tent under the moon and stars. Boy was that a mistake! Within minutes, we were swarmed by what seemed like thousands of mosquitoes. I tried to continue making love but I was literally getting my ass chewed up so we went back into finish .We were done. We were laying there cuddling and something in my mind just snapped. Hell, for no reason whatsoever, I started crying uncontrollably. Maybe it was me hearing the crackling of the fire going, I am not certain, but the incident of the house fire I started entered my mind. At that moment, I was feeling so guilty for the burns I caused my mother and brother, as well as for all that pain and heartache I put them through. Heather asked what was wrong and I told her. She tried her best to comfort and console me, but everything she was saying fell on deaf ears. To make matters worse, I felt embarrassed to be bawling my eyes out in front of her. I must have cried for at least three hours that night until I fell asleep .We never spoke on that incident again.

"There were sometimes Heather and I had inconsequential disputes and would spend days apart. I'd hang with a buddy named Mark, who lived not far from my house. He was an extreme pot-head and spent a lot of time playing PlayStation. I liked spending time at his house 'cause his mom was a pot-head, and so she didn't care if we blazed in the house. So we would just get stoned and play PlayStation all day. Heather and I were going through one of our disputes when my parents decided they wanted to take us kids to Chicago for the weekend to see the Bulls play the Milwaukee Bucks, and to go to some museums. Instead of taking Heather, I asked if Mark could come with us. My parents agreed and we went on our trip. At the hotel, Mark and I got stoned then waited until late night to go to the arcade. While playing in the arcade, we decided to break into the machines and steal the quarters so we could play all night. So, we got a crowbar from my parents' car and pried off the locks of about seven or eight machines, stealing all the quarters.

"We ended up with about $200 worth of quarters. When

we got back home, we used every penny of that money to buy a fat-ass sack of weed. That night, we went through 15 blunts and countless rolling papers. I was straight stuck on stupid. We continued to hang out from time to time, but eventually I moved on to another crowd.

"Juanito's mom threw a birthday party for his sister, so Heather and I went to the party. By then, I had already started slinging[4] weed for pocket change and had a little cash on me. I bought a few bottles of liquor for everyone and we got twisted. Juanito's mom Carmen had left to go get something from the store. While she was gone, I was sitting on the window ledge in Juanito's room drinking, when of all of a sudden I find myself falling in the air. As I was falling to what I assumed would be my death, since it was from the second floor window, I was facing the sky and noticed the entire window frame and window was floating right above me. I hit the ground, landing on a grassy area on my back, and the window frame and window landed right on top of me. I blacked out for a minute. When I came back to, Juanito and Heather were both running out of the house to check on me. At that same moment, Carmen was arriving home in a taxi. As I was lying there looking up at the big hole I left in her house, I went into a panic thinking she was going to be pissed at me. I jumped up so fast and dragged the window frame to the side of the house like I needed to hide it. I thought Carmen wouldn't notice the huge hole in her house. I wasn't thinking too clearly at the time 'cause of all the alcohol I had drank. She immediately saw what happened and Juanito told her. I was more concerned whether or not I was hurt rather than a hole. Amazingly I wasn't hurt other than a few cuts and bruises. It probably helped a great deal that I was drunk. My back has had problems ever since that incident.

"Mom went on a work-related vacation for a week leaving us kids by ourselves with our step-dad. Every time she wasn't around; he would use that time to get drunk. During this occasion, he did the same. Juanito and Heather were staying the night when an older neighbor kid talked me into stealing my parent's car. My stepdad passed out drunk that night and we took the car to go cruising. I let Jason drive 'cause he was the oldest. We cruised around for a while until the car broke down. Jason's dumb ass had been driving in a second overdrive the whole time, which caused the car to break down. He ended up leaving to supposedly call someone to get help -- but never came back. We didn't know what to do; it was like *damn*, so we went to sleep in the car. In the morning, we woke up to the police calling us out of the car and arresting us. Step-dad noticed the car gone and had reported it stolen. So us kids sat at the jail for a few hours till my step-dad showed up with Heather's mom. He was pissed and wanted to press charges but Dina had talked him out of it. So we all got released .The car was shot to hell. I never did tell my parents about Jason or it being him that fucked up their car."

PLUGS AND BLUNTS: ADOLESCENCE[5]

On the streets, Miles and his friends had found an alternative to the homes that were filled with drunken, racist step-dads, mothers who lost custody of their children, fathers who walked out on their mothers, parents who couldn't –or wouldn't –find jobs and pay their rent. They found groups like the Shorty Folk and the 2-1's that gave them a sense of security in a world where there never seemed to be enough food, enough money or enough love. The gangs provided it all. They said, "This is our block. We're keeping it." "This is our food. We're taking it." Anything they needed the gangs took and shared. It was a cruel, basic world where life "ain't nothing but bitches and money" – and respect. It was a world where there was so little that if you disrespected a guy by stepping on his brand-new sneakers, you could get killed; if you "got slick" with your mouth in someone else's neighborhood, then you might get "popped."

The gods of their world were symbols of power like Scarface, the fictional Cuban cocaine dealer who goes down with guns blazing against an army of DEA agents; the OG's (Original Gangsters who founded the gang crews in the area) were respected because they had survived the wars and made it possible for them to have something – anything – in this Hobbesian world. They admired "thugs" who could walk into enemy territory and, with impunity, regain stolen goods: "Tim was a huge guy who looked kind of like the Bald Bull who would always crush dudes on that game, Nintendo. One time I was using my grandfather's bike, taking it for a ride, when someone stole it from the back yard. Brad and I walked the 'hood looking for it, and came across three or four kids who had it. And we approached them to get the bike back; they told us if we wanted the bike we had to fight for it. Brad told them we would be back with one of our buddies. We left and got Tim. When we got back, the three kids, they seen us coming and whistled real loud. From up in the park behind them, about 30 black kids came running at us. Tim just looked at me and said for me to get out of there and he and Brad would handle them. Tim literally knocked out the first four who ran up on him. He and Brad stood back to back and were knocking down and slamming them on the ground just as fast as they were coming. They took their lumps too, of course, but I was really amazed at how well they stood their ground against those odds. The sheriffs came down the road which ended the fight. They didn't even stop. After it was broken up, the biggest black dude walked up to us and shook our hands. He said that he'd never seen white boys with so much heart before and there wouldn't be any war. I took my grandfather's bike back home and that was that."

They looked up to pimps who strolled along collecting money from women who sold themselves for their benefit. "That's how you hustle," they said to themselves. "That's how you handle your business." They would even recreate themselves when they finally got "jumped into" a gang by taking a new name and marking themselves with tattoos that symbolized their allegiance to this new and powerful entity. They shed their Christian names given to them in a church or at the hospital while their father was out in the waiting room. They were rechristened with names that showed how hard, how dangerous and how slick they were – a signal to the streets that these cold-hearted warriors were to be reckoned with carefully. Michael was given the name Blades, which he proudly "tagged" with spray paint in enemy turf.

Basically, if it was on their turf and in their 'hood, they felt it belonged to them. They stole for spending money; they stole to get high; they stole for fun; and sometimes, like in Miles' case, they just stole and didn't even know why half the time: "Spending so much time at Heather's house, I started meeting people in that area. One night I hit the gas station up to get blunts and this yellow kid[6] my age with an orange 'fro started trying to sell me a sack of weed when I came out of the store. Kid's name was Jonah but everyone knew him as Lucky. I bought a dime sack from him and matched him a blunt. He was a cool dude, funny as hell, and only lived three blocks from Heather's. We started hanging out on a regular basis and getting into all types of shit we had no business doing. His sister was dating a Jamaican guy who was pushing major weight[7] on the weed tip[8]. Jonah would sell weed for him just so he could smoke all the time for free.

"We got off into scams that we called "plugs." If one of us knew someone working at any type of store, we would holler at that person and find ways to scam the stores hour of whatever we could. Jonah had this chick who worked at Walgreen. We would go to her job and take a few $100 worth of items to her check-out register. She would scan all the items then void them so the alarm wouldn't sound when we left. For the cameras, we would pay for one of the item. We had another plug with the dude at K-mart, where he would have us bring things to his register and he would list the items as returns -- getting us in-store credit. Another plug we had with a dude at a Wal-Mart where he did inventory and would steal DVD and PlayStation games and sell them to us for $5.00 each .We were always hustling and finding ways to get cash.

"Jonah introduced me to a kid named Nick who lived a block from Heather's. Nick's uncle pushed coke, so he had access, and we started snorting lines occasionally. First time I did coke I could not sit still or stop talking to save my life. Although it was a high I enjoyed, I didn't do it often.

"Nick had robbed a house, stealing a few guns. Three of us would shoot them off in a nearby field. I forget exactly what happened, but I remember going to detention center and doing a few months because of them guns. Nick got knocked off for the burglary he did, and that was the last time we hung with him.

"My parents ended up getting evicted from our house because our landlady was a crack head. She got herself in a financial situation, then needed the house because she had no place else to stay herself. To add insult to injury that bitch pulled a real junkie stunt and sued my parents, claiming we caused damage to her house. The foundation was cracked due to a damn school bus smashing into the corner of the house when we lived there. My grandparents had moved to 101st Street, which was only about a mile away. We had no place else to go, so we'd moved in with them. Brad lived six blocks away, so I started hanging with them every day again. My grandparents' house was huge but it only had three bedrooms. James shared a room with my parents and I shared a room with Heather. She didn't officially live with us, but she was there most of the time. There were a few neighborhoods kids we hung with on a regular basis. It was Tim who dated a girl named Nicole. There was Barbara who had a little brother named Ray. And there was another girl named Kail. Tim had all kinds of connections on drugs. He and Brad stopped by one night and asked if I wanted to buy a couple of hits of acid, and I never did acid so I figured I would try it out. I got two hits thinking maybe I could get Heather to trip with me. Heather wasn't into using any drugs, smoking cigarettes, or even drinking anything other than wine coolers.

"Heather and I had just come from the pet store .We bought a salamander. I figured I'd wait until later before popping the acid, 'cause if my parents were in bed, I'd feel more comfortable. Heather told me straight up she wasn't doing no acid. I thought about dropping a hit in her soda, but I decided against that. I started sucking and chewing on both hits as soon as my parents were getting ready to go to their room. About 25 minutes had passed and I still wasn't feeling any different. Heather decided she wanted to go to Wal-Mart in order to get a tank, gravel and other crap for the salamander. Our car was broken down so she called her mom for a ride. Soon as she knocked, I started feeling the acid taking effect. I was laughing at everything that was said, even though I shouldn't have been 'cause they were arguing. Heather noticed immediately and started helping me try to maintain in front of her mom. When we got inside Wal-Mart, all the light had me dazed in awe. Everything looked crazy to me and I wanted to touch everything. We got what we needed and got back home pretty fast. Heather sent me in the bathroom to wash off the rocks for the fish tank, and I probably would have stayed there all night had she not come to get me.

"When I put my hands in the water, they looked like they were bubbling up and melting away. I filled the sink up and I literally stuck my whole head in the washer and started blowing bubbles. I had forgotten about the rocks and finally Heather came in and checked on me after 20 minutes or so. She cleaned the rocks then put them inside the tank. While she did that, I messed around with the salamander. For some reason, I felt like I needed to have water on my head in order to survive. So every 10 minutes or so, I would dunk my head in this tank. Finally, Heather got me a rag and bucket of water so I could keep the water on my head.

"That was a crazy night for me. Another time, Brad came over and he had some mushrooms. Everyone was gone from the house. We ate about a ¼ of 'shrooms each. He ended up leaving to go someplace when they started kicking in. Shit had me tripping hard. I was lying in my room on the bed and my room's real clean and organized. I had this cartoon poster of the Tasmanian devil on my wall and one of Bugs Bunny. Next thing I know the Tasmanian devil came off the poster and did his tornado spin all around my bedroom, trying to mess up all of my belongings. Bugs Bunny jumped out the poster saying, "What's up Doc? Looks like you need to clean." After that I convinced myself to close my eyes and sleep that shit off.

"A few months later, a guy named Ray and I stole a moped motor bike. Didn't work at the time but Ray was a whiz at fixing motors and had it running in no time. A few days after having it, some kids from those apartments ran up on us to get their moped back. Kids wanted to beef, but realized since we fixed it and since they got it back there was no harm, no foul. Ray and I were always stealing dirt bikes, go carts -- anything with an engine. I stole a go-cart, which Ray fixed up real good. That thing went about 60 miles per hour. We started taking turns driving around the block .While it was my turn to go, a dammed cop tried me and blocked off the road with his truck .There was a little space between his bumper and the curb. He was standing in the road waving at me to stop. I slowed down like I was stopping and right when I got to the truck, I smashed the gas and went through that little gap. I hit it so hard I was probably home before he even got his truck moved. I ended up storing the go cart at Heather's moms and we stopped messing with that stuff for a while."

"I went on another hunting trip with my grandfather. This time something happened that ended up changing everyone's life in my family. Heather and I stayed in the hotel room while everyone else went to the bar. So we opened the window to be able to hear if anyone was coming. There was a payphone out by our window and we heard grandpa talking on the phone. He was having phone sex with the person he was talking to. I realized then he was cheating on my grandma. When we got back home from our trip I told my grandma what had happened. She suspected it for years and finally confronted him. They decided to split up after being together for over thirty years. My grandpa lived with us after that for a few months. During that time, I started cheating around on Heather and slept with this girl from school named Casey. That was the absolute worst lay ever known to mankind. I was so drunk and high when I left her house and got home I realized I was still wearing the condom. When we were fucking the girl just lay there like a damned doll or something. I thought maybe it was because of the weed or the alcohol or something, but it wasn't. I know because I ended up hitting it later down the line and it wasn't any better sober. She had a little sister and friend who would beg me to fuck them, but I never would. I've never been into chicks younger than me.

"Juanito heard we would be moving soon and asked me to spend the night at my place to catch up. When he came over, he said we needed to talk 'cause he had something important to tell me. Long story short, he came out of the closet and told me he was bisexual. Shit blew my mind 'cause he was a good-looking guy that all the girls were always after. The news didn't change nothing between us. The night he stayed over we snuck out and he took us to a bisexual bar. We were both many years underage but we still got in. I was hesitant on being there because I didn't know what to expect. I have no interest in men so I figured I'd just be drinking while he did his socializing. To my surprise there were a bunch of females there also. There was a pretty little chick, about 26, who introduced herself to me and we just clicked. So I spent my time hanging with her. She bought me some drinks and we danced together to some songs. The way she was grinding her ass up against my dick made want her in the worst way. When the bar closed, I asked her for a ride home. She gave me her keys and had me drive. When we arrived at home, she said goodbye to Juanito and starting kissing me. I started trying to talk her into letting us come to her house 'cause I really wanted to hit that pussy. But she had to work and we could get together another time. She left and we snuck back into the house without anyone ever knowing we were gone.

"The next day Juanito went back home and we never really hung out again. Never really knew why either. I wound up getting into some bullshit with some kid and the dude called the police on me. I was shocked as Hell when the police arrested me for strong-arm robbery. The dude lied and said I stole his wallet. I went to the detention center and did a few months. While I was there my parents and brother moved in with my cousin Mary Jane back on the South Side. Grandma moved in with my cousin on 74th street and Lisbon. Grandpa moved in with his girl he had been cheating on grandma with for over 15 years.

He let my grandma keep everything except his clothes and his van. He even continued to give her money. When I was locked up, grandpa would visit me almost every weekend and give me books to read. Heather had packed all my stuff, since I wasn't home to do it, and she stored everything at her house.

"I found myself getting into plenty of fights. A lot of them were over next to nothing. I have a slick-ass mouth and ain't afraid to speak my mind. And back then I was quick to swing on anyone if I felt they disrespected me in any way. I even had beef with the correctional officers. There was one who used to send kids to beat me up. But none that he sent ever could beat me down. I was a scrawny-ass kid but the majority of my fights I would knock the kid down or out with only one punch. Till this day, I've never lost a heads-up fight. Came close once with a kid the guard sent at me. We were at rec. playing ball and for no reason at all this kid sweeps my legs out from under me. When I hit the ground, the kid started pounding on me. I managed to get back on my feet and return some blows. The guards broke it up as soon as I got some blows in.

"At that exact moment, they took me to the visitation room because my grandma was there to see me. I wasn't looking too bad. Only had a knot on the back of my head and fat, busted lip. Fucked up part was I always got put on cell restriction for my fights and the other kids didn't. Hell, the guards would give them extra food trays and special privileges for fighting me. Fighting didn't bother me, though. My cuz Paul and I use to box each other on the streets for money all the time. So, for me, fighting was just a part of regular life.

"I got out of the detention center and was sentenced to do probation. It couldn't have been two weeks I was out before I was arrested again. The same damned kid made a report to the police that I threatened him. Shit had me real bitter because I never even seen the kid again after the first incident. I did a few months in the detention center and then was transferred to a lower security center. They transferred me late so when I arrived at the new place, it was bed time. I slept that night and the next morning I was already making plans to haul ass form that place. They were letting us out for rec. and I took off running for the woods. Another kid ran with me. I looked back and he was so far behind I decided to run back for him. I grabbed his arm and pretty much dragged him as I ran. We got away with no problems. I never knew the kid's name. I just called him Lil Bit because he was a short black kid who weighed a little bit of nothing. We walked so far we ended up at the state fair a few miles away. Neither of us had any money so we snuck into the fair grounds and started stealing these huge stuffed animals from the game booths. Between the two of us we must have stolen 30 of these stuffed animals. They were really easy to sell for 10 or 15 dollars apiece, because people were spending way more than that trying to win them at the game booths. I ain't sure how much money we made that day, but we left with almost 300 dollars, and we spent a load of money at the fair. We had a lot of fun going on the rides and eating food.

"When the fair closed we left with a huge bag of stuffed animals and took a cab to my mom's house. She was living on 20th and Scott with my cousin Mary Jane and her kids. Nobody was surprised I ran from the center and that I had company with me. First thing I did was trying to find someone to buy a quarter pound of weed. I ran into my ex-Haley's brother, Jerry, and he said he could get what I needed. I trusted him and gave him 250 dollars to go get the weed. But 20 minutes after he left, a 2-1 named Smurf stopped by. I wanted a sack to smoke while I was waiting on Jerry, so I asked Smurf about a dime bag. I gave him 10 dollars to go get a bag down the street. I must have waited four hours before it really sunk in that both these dudes done beat me out my money. I was disappointed but I had that easy-come –easy-go mentality.

"We ended up crashing there for the night. The next morning Lil Bit, my cuz Toya and I decided we were gonna steal a car. We took a screwdriver and walked a few blocks from the house until we came across a nice-looking old Cadillac. After I busted the back window out, it took me about five minutes to get it started. They both hopped in and I drove to an alley on 20th. Everyone wanted to drive, but I didn't trust either of them knew how. Lil Bit swore he could drive even though he could barely reach the pedals and see out the windows. I decided to give him a chance but without Toya and me in the car. He got in the driver's seat and was only going to drive around the block. When he pulled off, Toya and I were joking that he would crash before he got back to us. A few minutes passed and Lil Bit was coming back down the alley hitting garbage cans. The police were right behind him. Toya and I both dipped when Lil Bit drove into a garage and jumped out the car. I went my own way and must have set some kind of record getting back to the house. I was peeking out the window when, about 10 minutes later, I see Toya walking up to the house and the police pulling up and stopping her. They had Lil Bit in the back seat and he was yelling and trying to say he knew Toya, he didn't do nothing, and he was with her. She said she was coming from her grandma's a few blocks down and didn't know the kid; they left with Lil Bit and Toya came in the house. We were both really relieved that we weren't in that car while he was driving.

"I ended up turning myself into my probation officer soon after that. Not for that incident though. The police kept stopping by my mom's house because I escaped from the center. I just wanted to get all that mess over with. They put me in another group home. I was there about four days before I got into trouble. One of the kids blamed me for something he did and I was put on restriction. I said fuck this, and hauled ass out a window. I went to Heather's to stay there. Probation officer calls mom and tells her that if she speaks to me to tell me if I turn myself in within 72 hours, I won't receive any more charges. Mom contacted me and told me her news. Heather talked me into turning myself in so I wouldn't get into anymore trouble. So I turned myself in and went back to the detention center."

LAD LAKE

Lad Lake motto (1917): "To cure is the voice of the past. To prevent is the Divine Whisper of today."

Lad Lake has been a Wisconsin institution since the early 20th century. At first, it was called the Wisconsin Home and Farm School because it was actually a working farm. Labor was supposed to redeem the wayward boys who were sent there and who needed to learn the values of hard work and responsibility. To this day, the grounds are located about a half-an-hour drive outside of Milwaukee in a town called Dousman; it extends over 367 acres of land. To a kid used to houses crammed "side-by-side" and streets packed with cars and debris, the place must seem majestic.

By the time Miles was a resident at Lad Lake, not much had changed. The mission of the place was to "provide a brighter future" for kids who came from troubled families and from the streets that offered no future. The latest version of the facility added a complete panel of services from one-on-one classroom attention, to behavioral counseling or "simply being a shoulder to cry on." Lad Lake boasts of being the "next step" in creating success in previously unsuccessful young people. As in the early days of the institution, the boys were still expected to work, to learn and to be physically healthy – but the type of resident had changed. There was a meaner, inner-city edge to the kids who came out to the country, and they carried this attitude to the bucolic setting of Lad Lake.

In January 2000, Miles obtained his GED, and had passing test scores. A teacher described a pattern in Miles' school grades: "Well, his attendance, when I looked at whenever he was absent from school, the final grade was lower, nonexistent. When he attended school and there was [sic] no absences, his grades were actually in the B and C range." At Lad Lake, Miles improved his reading level two grade levels in six months.

In 1998, this same teacher detailed some of Miles' other scores: "[H]is scores are at least of an average student or a little better. Um, Algebra C; Biology C ; Career Studies C; English 10, that would be tenth grade English, B+; um, I believe, LEAP, it's a program 22 possibly for at risk students may be, B; Phys. Ed B; and U.S. history was incomplete." She saw nothing of Miles that would indicate that he had severe brain damage, and she saw nothing that would suggest that he was mentally retarded.

For many, such as Miles, Lad Lake was another step in the life-long process of institutionalization, wherein the individual becomes more a product of the institution's culture and loses his original identity. The educational opportunity is lost in the haze of restrictions, the steel bars – both visible and invisible – and the regulations that become a way of life. After a while, there is only *locked up* or *not locked,* nothing in between; no other mentality. So, the education these kids get in places like this is not just what is drummed into their heads during class time, but it is also a primer course in how to smuggle in stuff like tobacco and candy, how to defend yourself with your fists and how to keep in contact with the outside world; in other words, how to function in "kiddy jail." This was the first step in Miles' *institutionalization*: "After a few months I went in front of the judge and was sentenced to complete a program at Lad Lake Group Home. Lad Lake was a huge piece of land set up kind of like a summer camp. There were several different cottages to house kids. There was a school house, a full football field, a rec. center, and a lake on the grounds. I wasn't that excited to be there but it didn't seem like all that bad a place to be. I was housed in a cottage with 23 other kids. The rooms were regular bedrooms with 2 beds, 2 desks, and 2 closets. We were allowed to bring pretty much anything we wanted from home like clothes, jewelry, hygiene, radio, etc. ... if we didn't have nothing, they provided it. Every day we had to do chores and we got paid for them every week. They had three different levels of phases a kid would be on. You start off on phase one and you can earn your way up to Phase Two and Three by showing improvement in different areas. On phase 2 or 3 a kid could go on weekend passes to go home on weekends. There were other privileges too like getting to stay up later, going off grounds, make more allowance etc. ... Monday through Friday we had to go to school. After school, we could go to the rec. building for about an hour. The rec. building had a pool table, dart board, TV and a canteen window where we could buy all kinds of snacks. Or we could go to the football field and play or just walk around. After the rec. we would go back to the cottage and have group therapy. We were expected to open up about our feelings and accept constructive criticism. Every meal we all would eat together. Food was great and we could eat as much as we wanted. Each day we would have to do individual counseling with a therapist for about thirty minutes or an hour. There was a TV room where we could watch TV after dinner. We could also go back to the rec. room or the football field, go fishing on the lake or just chill in our rooms. There were showers we could use any time we wanted. There was a phone we were allowed to use once a week to talk to our family. One of the staff use to take us on nature walks in the woods pretty often. That was always fun.

"After describing the place it almost sounds like a resort, but actually it was a lot of hard work. The place was designed to teach us discipline, educate us, give us structure, and provide us the tools needed to become productive members of society. About once a month my parents would come in so we could have family therapy and work on issues at home. I could also earn time when people could come spend time with me. My mom and Heather came together a lot of times. When they did, I would usually sit in the car with them to talk. Really, mom would fall asleep and Heather and I would have sex or fool around. One of the staff used to do volunteer work in the community feeding the homeless, taking care of farm animals etc. ... she would always let 5 or 6 of us go with her to help, if we wanted to, and had been good. I went as often as possible. Not only did I enjoy doing the stuff and getting off grounds for a while, but it was also a time we could easily get opportunities to smoke. Of course, we smoked on grounds too but we were always having to look over our shoulder while on grounds. Cigarettes were easy to come by. Every time I had a visit, I had my people bring me a few packs, even though they weren't allowed. It was either that or have to pay a dollar per cigarette on the black market. Instead of being one of the kids buying cigarettes, I decided to sell them. Each week allowance came as I was collecting every dime all the kids made. I never had beef with any of the kids and got along with everyone there.

"Several months had gone by and I had made it to Phase Two right before X-Mas. My mom was still living on 20th with my cousin Mary Jane and her kids. By this time my lil' brother James had moved away to live with my cuz Nicole. Haley and her boyfriend Bobo got relocated there under protective custody by the feds. Bobo was a 2-1 and some shit happened where another 2-1 killed a family member or close friend of his. He turned state witness and they had to be relocated. When I got to my mom's I didn't have a room or any stuff 'cause it was all at

Heather's. The place had roaches so bad I was scared to even sit down some place let alone sleep there. I spent the day there and ended up drinking and getting smoked out on some good green with some family. There was no way I was gonna sleep in that house, so I took the bus to Heather's that night. I spent the rest of my weekend with her; we mainly watched movies together and made love.

"After my weekend was over, I went back to Lad Lake where they surprised me with a urine test. I failed my test and got dropped back down to Phase One. About a month later, my grandpa, mom, step dad and Heather came to visit me. My visit was supposed to be confined to the building, but when they arrived I went outside to greet them. When we came back inside Heather told me she had something important to talk to me about right when a staff member came and cancelled car visit due to me going outside to greet them. Of course, I was .38 hot and started going off. Heather gave me two greeting cards before they left and I was still going off. The staff ended up putting me in a padded, locked room until I was ready to cool down. For about 20 minutes, I kicked the door until my feet hurt and I was worn out. I realized I still hadn't read the card Heather gave me, so I pulled them out my pocket and started reading them. The first card I read said something like "congratulations on being a dad." I was so confused. After reading what she wrote in the second card, it finally dawned on me that she was pregnant and that was the important thing she had wanted to walk about. I was only 15 years old, so I'd be lying to say I wasn't scared. But I was also happy and excited. I told my counselor about it and we had a family counseling session. I was scared to tell my mom and decided to tell my step-dad first. He let me know that they already knew 'cause Heather had already told them. Still it was hard for me to talk to her about it. She was actually excited, though she wished it hadn't happened so soon. Heather wanted to take parenting classes and I thought that was a good idea. I asked permission to be able to attend the classes with her off grounds once a week. They allowed my grandpa to pick me up every week and take me to the classes with Heather. I got a 5-hour off-grounds pass. I could continue with the classes as long as I wasn't gone longer than the five hours. Grandpa would pick us up, drop us off; and then pick us up when it was over. I usually still had an hour or longer to hang out with Heather and grandpa after the class was done. There was only five other people taking the class with us. I took the classes seriously and tried learning everything possible. The group home psychiatrist had diagnosed me with ADHD and I started taking a medication called Ritalin and another pill to help me sleep. I guess the medications helped because they saw an improvement in me once I started taking them. Every now and then I would crush up the Ritalin and snort it to get high."

There is an old saying on the streets that "Any fool with a dick can have a baby, but it takes a man to be a father." Of course, this means that anyone can create the kid but it takes a lot of strength, patience and endurance to stick around through a whole lifetime of raising a kid. It also takes a lot of money and maturity. It doesn't hurt to come from a strong, consistent family background. Miles had been reared by a drunken, racist step-father and did not get to know his biological father until much later in life. His mother's biological father was incarcerated and, according to what she heard, was shot during an escape attempt. Miles' own biological father was a convict who was bi-polar and was elusive to his sons though most of their young lives. Miles, willingly or not, inherited these traits: the unstable psychology, the intermittent attempts at fatherhood and the brushes with the law. Thus, Miles didn't really have much in his favor when he became a father – no experience, nothing more than classroom training in how to raise a child, no steady money, no job and a fractured education.

Miles, who was supposed to have been educated in the ways of the "productive citizen" at Lad Lake, fell back into his old hustles when back on the streets of Milwaukee. He refined his skills as a thief and attained almost legendary proportions.

All the while, he stayed as high and as drunk as possible: "I completed the program at Lad Lake and got released. I moved in with Heather, her sister Rachel, and her mother Dina. My mom and step-dad ended up getting their own place to rent back in the same side-by-side houses we got kicked out of, right off 107th and Brown Deer Road. They had three bedrooms and were only using one so Heather and I moved in with them. We had one room and my mom turned the other room into the baby's room. She went all out on the room, buying everything for the room. She even painted it and put up cartoon stenciling around the border. It turned out great. Mom always loved Heather as her own daughter. But Heather really didn't enjoy living with my mom. Heather is a spoiled brat and not used to having or following any rules. Mom is very blunt and speaks her mind. Mom didn't have any rules really. She only asked for us to keep our radio down. For us, that was an impossible task. Heather and I spent a lot of our days watching rented movies, playing video games or going to the movies. One time we went out to the movies at a theater not far from the house. She must have been about 7 months pregnant at the time. When we left the movies, I decided to drive us home. On the way home, we had the radio on and it was hitting real hard 'cause we had an amp and subs in the trunk. I ended up getting pulled over because of the radio noise. Since I didn't have a license and Heather did, we tried to switch seats before the cop got to our car. The cop didn't even go to her door. He went straight to the passenger door cause he seen us switch seats. He searched our car and he found a weed pipe that I forgot was in the glove compartment. He gave me several tickets and said if my girl wasn't pregnant I would have been going to jail.

"Heather had been working at a Little Caesar's pizza place not far from her mom's house. She had become assistant manager and told me to apply for a job there. The manager Mike really liked Heather, knew her situation and hired me on the spot. Mike was a great boss to have. He expected us to work hard, but we got to have fun too. Some nights, he would bring a full bottle of liquor to work and we would start drinking about an hour before closing time. Before I left work, I'd be twisted. We had another assistant manager that smoked weed. I'd get her blowed and she would let me do whatever I wanted. She didn't care if I gave away free food, sold weed – nothing. I had a lot of fun at that job.

"The day Heather went into labor she woke me up at 7 am. We went to the hospital. Her sister and my parents waited in the waiting room while Dina and I stayed with Heather. I was more excited than anything else. I hated seeing Heather in pain during the contractions and the birth but she took it like a champ. During the delivery I held her hand and wiped the sweat from her head. Soon as our son Austin was born the doctor wiped him off and did the weighing and other stuff. When he tried handing Austin to Heather, she told him to give him to me. I was filled with so much joy and pride that I thought I'd bust. I held our son and talked to him. I gave him to Heather and went to announce the news to everyone else. It was a few days before Heather and Austin were released from the hospital. I stayed with Heather most of that time. The hospital gave me a bracelet so that I could get our son from the baby room any time I wanted. When they were released Heather went straight to her mom's and moved back in with her. I was upset because she didn't even discuss it with me -- and because my mom did so much to welcome the baby into our house already. I moved in with them right away. We turned Heather's room into the baby's room and the basement was ours. Between the baby shower, my parents, my grandparents, her parents, and family, we had enough baby stuff for several kids. We had three baby cribs, several strollers, car seats, bouncers, and so much more. We had to take a lot back to the stores 'cause we didn't need it all. We didn't like running upstairs every time Austin cried so we had him sleep in a bassinette next to our bed. Heather started back at work pretty much right away. We would have our schedules set so that one of us would always be free to watch Austin. Dina or

Rachel never had a problem watching for us any time we needed or asked. Things went pretty smooth in the house for a while.

"X-mas time came around and we went to Chicago to spend it with Heather's family. Rachel brought her boyfriend Matt who I got along with really well, probably because he drank and liked to do the same drugs as me. Not only that but he's funny and entertaining too. Dina never came with us because that was their dad's side of the family. Everyone was real friendly, and nice to both Matt and I. Matt is a few years older than me so they didn't mind him drinking even though he was still under age. I spent a lot of time hanging in the garage where everyone had to go to smoke cigarettes only 'cause I could drink in there and I felt more comfortable in there. Matt and I would go to his car a lot to smoke weed. Overall, it was a fun time.

"Back at home, some time had passed. I was sitting on the porch and Jonah pulled up sitting in the passenger seat of a car. He told me to jump in the back so we could blaze a blunt. When I got in, I noticed the driver was someone I seen at the parenting class. He was introduced to me and we were both surprised to live only three blocks from each other. His name was Jason and he was a twenty-year-old white kid that was ghetto as fuck. I liked him right from the start. We smoked out[9] that day and started hanging out all the time, mostly at his house, 'cause his wife Hope was always trippin' about him being gone all the time. His dad owned a duplex three blocks from our house. Jason, Hope and their daughter lived downstairs. Jason's sister Valerie lived upstairs with her own daughter, Latecia. Valerie is about 1 and-a-half years older than me and fine as hell. Their dad lived in the basement and was hardly ever seen. They also had an older brother named Steve who lived on his own and had his own daughter. Through Jason I met a few older guys that we pretty much kicked it with every day. There was a guy called Yo who lived about six blocks from us. There was a black dude who loved to go by the name Little John that I had a love for. Then there was this mixed dude named Chuck that was in and out of prison.

"On weekends we would all go out together to bars. Since I was underage, they would only go to places they could get me in at. Mostly we just got drunk and shot pool. We would all hang at Jason's and smoke ourselves stupid and play Playstation. Jason and I got real tight. He would drive us around every day to every store possible. It was mostly me doing the stealing but he would pocket little shit. I don't know how it happened but I got straight out of control and off the chain on what we called our 'missions' of stealing. I was so good at stealing that I felt there was nothing that couldn't be got if I put my mind to it. I didn't care about security, cameras, and alarm devices on stuff – none of that stopped me. If anything it was a challenge I was up to. I had nerves of steel and would steal shit right in front of anyone and they wouldn't even have a clue.

"I had different approach strategies for different stores or items. I always carried a razor palmed in my hand when going to stores. Anything that was in the hard plastic cases I would just use the blade to cut the item out. To avoid the cameras seeing this happen, I would carry two of the same items and cut the bottom one out, leaving the top one intact. I'd slide the item up my sleeve and then place both packages back on the shelf. For CD's, DVD's and video games I would always carry a flathead screwdriver to pop off hard casing that's holding the item in the with the alarm tab. If I wanted jewelry out of that plastic spinning case that are locked where people can spin the jewelry to see all the items that it holds inside, I would get creative. I'd find some kind of stick like bendable item in the store and slide it in through the crack by the spinning wheel. I'd use the stick like item to knock the jewelry off the hooks or boxes in there; then they would fall to the bottom of the spinner. I would just push down on the spinner to give myself a little extra room to use the stick like item to drag the jewelry out. Then I'd slip it up my sleeve.

"Anything that was nailed down as a model display I simply used a screwdriver to pry and bust it out. The display items like cameras that are hooked to a wire, and if removed the alarm goes off, I'd just cut the wire with my razor and when the alarm went off I'd act surprised. When the store employees check the items, they appear un-tampered with because the cord is still attached to the item. After they leave, I'd just take the item as well as the cut cord.

"Clothes that had ink tags that explode when not properly removed I would simply use another clothing item to wrap around it and then pop off the tag. That way the ink got on the one item and not the stuff I was stealing. Shoes, I would go in barefoot and walk out wearing stolen ones. At times, I would even go into the employee storage rooms to get the shoes.

"Sometimes, I would go to other places like Sam's club and pull other stunts. Every store has blind spots where there is no camera viewing a certain area. Usually it's in the mechanic area. At Sam's Club, I liked to get these huge bags of dog food. I'd open the bag a little so I could dump part of the food out some place in the store. Then I'd load the bag up with other items I wanted and seal the bag up with glue from the store. I'd pay for the dog food and walk out with hundreds of dollars worth of other stuff inside the bag.

"Doing this stuff was like a job to me. We would drive from store to store stealing. Some places I'd go inside with an empty store bag and fill it up. I did this a lot for colognes. I'd put a shirt on the bottom of the bag that I was stealing. Then I'd put 4 or 5 bottles of cologne on that shirt. I'd put another shirt on top of that and then another shirt. I'd put another shirt on top of that and then more cologne. Depending upon my mood, I'd usually have 4 to 7 layers of shirts and colognes and before I just walked right out of the store.

"Anything that was electronic or digital, I just had to have. Digital cameras, camcorders, recording devices, atlas guides, hand-held TV's, and everything else. I loved stealing walkie-talkies, electric razors, electric toothbrushes, paintball guns, and all types of other shit. I'd walk into stores and eat food and drink beverages like shit was supposed to be free. The crazy thing is I usually gave away most of the shit I stole to Jason and other friends. Of course, I'd sell stuff too, so I could have money for alcohol, drugs or partying. I loved buying stuff for Heather or just splurging money on pointless stuff.

"I came across a chrome.380 pistol from someone in the hood and picked it up for like 80 dollars. I was selling weed and doing a lot of dirt so I figured it was a necessity. I started getting into breaking into garages and cars real heavy. I'd get smoked out or drunk real heavy and not be able to sleep. So I'd go out at night and rob cars for car decks, amps, subs, TV's, rims, CD's, and whatever else I could find. I'd hit garages and steal tools, lawn mowers, weed whackers, snow plows and whatever else I thought I could sell. Every time I went out to do this I'd hit dozens of cars and garages up until the sun came up. I'd store everything in Heather's mom's garage, basement, or at Jason's house.

"I was known in the hood as the go-to man 'cause you could come to me for anything. If I didn't have it, I would go get it. Didn't matter if it was legal or not. One guy asked me for a patio set and a grill. I had to steal a damned truck just to steal the stuff he wanted. You know how a person who steals usually goes into the store to steal a couple of candy bars or something? Well not me. I had to have whole boxes of candy bars. That's the way I was. Most thieves would be happy to walk out of a store with a 700 dollar item like a digital camera and not get caught. I would be pissed at myself if I was only able to walk out with one item.

"Hope used to hate me coming over because I would talk Jason into going out and we would be gone all day and night. I gave him so much shit all the time that he never cared. My brother James came back and was staying with my mom. He always wanted me to stop by. One time, Brad and I stopped by and he was home alone. For some crazy reason, Brad and I decided that we wanted to rob my mom's neighbor. They weren't home so I did the same thing I did when I was younger and entered their house through my mom's attic crawl space. I let Brad in at the door. We stole a few things and then left.

"Later that night I was at home with my son, Heather and

her mom just chillin'. The police showed up just as I was getting off the phone with my mom. She had called to tell me they were on their way and had arrested James. He hadn't told them a damned thing, but they knew someone from my mom's house robbed them because they found a footprint on top of a dresser below the crawl space in their house. They had James in a squad car and said he was being charged and told them I was involved. It only took a moment to think things through and decide I had to get him out that mess. I didn't want him in any trouble especially since he didn't do shit. So I told the police straight up that he didn't tell them nothing and that he didn't break into that house. I told the cop I would tell him who did it if he let James go. They agreed and I told them I did it on my own."

THE FIRST TRIP TO FLORIDA

I kept driving and Brad asked where we were going for real. I told him to Florida and that's when everyone realized I was serious. I asked if they wanted me to turn around and everyone was like "fuck it I ain't [sic] got nowhere [sic] to be." None of us had any money, but that didn't register as any concern for any of us. We smoked blunt after blunt after blunt after blunt until there wasn't shit left to smoke. Between us all we had about 20 dollars.

ANGEL MILES

When young people grow up seeing eviction letters posted on their front doors, parents coming and going in and out of jail, moving from one part of town to the next, with no stability for the days and months to come, there is no real sense of the future. There is no planning and no hope for security in the days ahead.

When these same kids grow up running the streets, or seeing their homes burn down with all their worldly belongings inside, or they wake up to find their houses burglarized of anything of value, or they find out after school their being placed in foster homes because their parents are going to "detox" from drugs, there is no sense of the past. The toys from Christmas, the snapshots from the park during childhood, the Little League trophies, and all the memories disappear over and over again. The past fades.

These street kids are left to reconstruct – over and over again – a sense of form in their lives, or at least material comfort. Thus, "life" boils down to the clothes on their backs, the hard cash in their pockets, the steel pistol that they keep to protect what they have, the friends who have "their back" in gang fights and the chicks who hang with them. It is all *here and now* – no future and no past. It's all about getting "yours" and getting their "respect" – in the moment.

Impulsivity festers.

The moment must be seized while the goods are there to be taken – they might disappear. Consequences for the future cannot be considered; punishments from the past mean nothing. It's all right here and now. They say, "Fuck it," and like a magical mantra has been uttered, all considerations outside the moment disappear. A car is stolen just for fun, to joy ride through the 'hood to show off to the other kids; new sneakers are flaunted at the park and fights erupt when someone steps on them during a basketball game ("Motherfucker steppin' on my New Air Jordans. I'll cap his ass next time I see that fool"); stolen jewelry is handed out to "honeys" so they believe they are living "ghetto fabulous." Some stuff is sold to have money for drugs or booze to get high on for a little while.

When the last of the weed is smoked, the last sip of liquor is drunk and the clothes are ripped and the sneakers are scuffed, the moment of glory is over. All the gold is gone; nothing left to glitter. "Fuck it," they say; "let's go get some more." They go to other stores with newer, better schemes for robbing them to get new stuff.

In Miles' case, not only did he live completely in the moment, say "fuck it," whenever he might have thought of consequences in the future; but Miles had to take it to the next level. He had to up the ante like a compulsive gambler; to make the moment shine brighter and be more intense than the last: "Brad got released and I got taken back to the detention center. I was there for some months and my lawyer told me because of my record I could be sentenced to boy's home until I turned 21. The state filed a motion to have me waved as an adult case 'cause I had just turned 17 or was about to. My lawyer said the judge would never agree to waive me and he would fight it.   I knew the system pretty well by then. I didn't want to get sentenced to no Boy's Home until I turned 21, and I didn't want to stay in no detention center fighting my charges. I was pretty certain if I was waived as an adult I would just get some probation, since it was my first adult charge. Plus, I knew I'd get a bail as an adult and could get out of jail right away.

"So against my lawyer's advice, I asked the judge to grant the state's motion to waive me as an adult. The judge did and that same day I was transferred to the county jail. At the county jail, I went in front of another judge and requested bail. I was given 1,000 dollars bail. I called my grandma and she put up the 1000 dollars and got me out. Down the line, I ended up being sentenced to probation with 2 [months] withheld and 2 9-month sentences. Meaning if I fucked up on probation, I could be sentenced to 18 months in jail.

"I was only on probation a short time before I fucked up again. My mom gave me a '91 Thunderbird that Heather mostly drove 'cause I had no license. The Fourth of July came around and Heather and I were going to go to the lake-front for the fireworks display with our son. I picked up a quarter-pound of weed to bag up and sell while down there. Well, it started to drizzle right as we were about to leave. Heather decided we weren't going. I wasn't trying to hear that shit. And I told her we were going. We got in an argument and I told her I was going with or without her. She started to protest. I told her it was my car and I would go if I wanted to. She threw the keys at me and I left.

"I picked up Brad and we decided to get Jonah too. We picked him up and this sexy-ass thick girl named Heidi. Said she wanted to come. Of course, I was quick to agree. I drove down to the lake front and parked. We rolled up several blunts and sat on the hood smoking and waiting for the display. Some time went by in which we blazed blunt after blunt before someone walking by asked if we were waiting on the display. We said, "Yeah."

Then they told us we they were doing the display on the 3rd and the 5th and not the 4th. We couldn't understand what sense that made but we ended up leaving.

"On the freeway we blazed more blunts. I rolled one for myself and one for them to pass around. We had the radio up and were clowning to the music while smoking. Brad told me we had missed our exit. I shrugged my shoulders and said I would catch the next one. I zoned off smoking my blunt and rapping with the music and missed the next one. Then Jonah said, 'Fuck it, keep driving.' I asked where we should go and everyone started joking and naming different states.

"Jonah said, 'Let's go to Florida,' and I said, 'Sounds good to me.' I kept driving and Brad asked where we were going for real. I told him to Florida and that's when everyone realized I was serious. I asked if they wanted me to turn around and everyone was like "fuck it I ain't got nowhere to be." None of us had any money, but that didn't register as any concern for any of us. We smoked blunt after blunt after blunt after blunt until there wasn't shit left to smoke. Between us all we had about 20 dollars.

"I just kept driving until we needed gas. We stopped at a gas station. All of us went in and stole food. Then before we left I filled up the gas tank and drove off without paying. We took turns driving. Heidi and I started getting and feeling a connection for each other. Her and I were sleeping in the back when we woke up to the car vibrating. The car blew a tire and Jonah was pulling off the road into a Cracker Barrel restaurant/store.

"It was an all-bad situation because I had no spare and we needed a whole new tire. I called my mom collect to try to figure something out. While I was on the phone Heidi and Jonah were hustling people for money and found a woman who was willing to help us. They gave her some story about going to Florida and running out of money; said family had money at Western Union waiting for us to pick up in Florida. The police pulled up and asked if we needed any help and everyone thought we were screwed. But they left after the lady said she was taking Heidi to get a tire. The woman bought us a tire and then gave us 40 dollars with an address to return it to her when we got to Florida. I believe we were in Kentucky at that time. We fixed the tire problem and got back on the road. Eventually we arrived on the border of Alabama and seen the ocean for the first time. We were all excited and wanted to hit the water.

"It was late at night and we were starving. I parked the car and we stole bread, cheese, lunch meat and mayo and we made sandwiches. We walked about a mile to the ocean and when we got there only 2 people were on the beach. It was an older white man and woman who called themselves drifters; said they had houses but often slept on beaches. They had a bottle of liquor and said we could use their blankets to lie on the sand and we could drink with them. So we were hanging out drinking with them in the middle of the night. I had a BB gun on me that I was using to shoot at things. Heidi and I decided to go into the ocean alone so we could be alone and fuck. We could barely see 10 feet in front of us but we went into the water. I swear we must have gone out at least 100 yards and the water was only past our waists. We had a good time fooling around, but didn't have sex because she said the salt water had her pussy feeling dried out. We went back to the beach and lay on the blanket to snuggle and drink. I passed out. Wasn't long before Heidi woke me up and I found myself being eaten alive by sand mites and red ants. I was no longer on the blanket. Heidi was frantic telling me the drifters yanked the blanket from underneath me and were going through something with Jonah and Brad.

"I found out Jonah was getting his dick sucked by the woman drifter when Brad walked over by them to see if he could get some head too. The woman got pissed and told him and his nigger friend could go to hell. Jonah was hot about the statement and they were all arguing. I grabbed Jonah and told

Brad and Heidi it was time to leave. We started walking up this hill and I guess the alcohol had got to everyone 'cause the drifters started coming after us. The guy ran up on Jonah and Jonah punched him in the face knocking him down the hill.

"Out of nowhere a car pulled up at the top of the hill and a skinny white guy and a huge black woman got out. The woman was the drifter's friend and heard her yelling at us when she got out of the car. The drifter woman was running at us and Jonah pushed her down the hill. Then the big black woman from the car started swinging on Jonah. They were going blow for blow until she kicked him in his balls. He went down and she was on top of him pounding away. I wasn't gonna let nobody beat on my homeboy, so I pulled out my BB gun and bashed her head with it. It dazed her enough so that Jonah could get up. Soon as he did, he started telling the woman why we were going through it with her friend. Once she heard her friend had called him a nigger, she wasn't mad at us anymore and everyone apologized for the fighting. They ended up giving us a ride to our car.

"We slept in the car that night. When we woke the next day, I drove us to Florida. We crossed this long-ass bridge going into Pensacola and had to stop at this tollbooth to pay a dollar. None of us had the money to pay it and the booth person had me pull to the side of the road. I tried to explain to him that had we known there was a toll to pay we would not have gone over it. I asked if we could just turn around but he said, "No." He told us to come up with what we could and he would be back. While he was gone we searched the car and only found 7 cents to give him. He came back and I gave him the change. He said that normally he was supposed to contact the sheriff for situations like ours, but he was gonna let us slide.

"So we arrived in Pensacola and hit the beach. There were people everywhere. Some older guys started to try to holler at Heidi, and I told her to take advantage of the situation. She did and had the guys buy us all some drinks. We bounced on the dudes as soon as we got them. All of us went swimming. None of us had ever seen or been to the ocean. So it was an amazing experience. Big schools of fish were swimming around everywhere. We caught a few shrimp and some crazy looking crabs in shells. It was a lot of fun for us all. We went back to the car to get some towels out the trunk where I noticed my complete tail light cover was missing. Right then, I knew we were going to have problems and was worried about being pulled over. We decided we were going to head home and on the way we planned to find another car like mine so we could steal the tail light cover.

"So, I started driving home. We figured if we had some money we could buy a cover at a junk yard if we couldn't find one to steal. So we started driving around and breaking into vehicles. I'd shoot out the window with the B.B. gun and we'd steal whatever we found. We did this all day long. We were still stealing when I pulled up in a store parking lot with a car in front of me and one on each side. We hit all three vehicles. When I put the car in reverse to pull out my car went forward smashing into the car in front of me. I checked to make sure the gear shift was in reverse and then hit the gas to pull out again. I knew something was seriously wrong and told everyone to get out and push my car backwards out of the parking spot. Once they did that, we hauled ass out of there. I found an empty street and tried the reverse gear again. Damned thing still went forward. I put it in neutral and when I hit the gas it went forward. None of us knew what was wrong. We just knew we couldn't reverse no more.

"We started heading home again and the speed limit was like 65 mph or something. My car wouldn't do more than 30 mph and started smoking. Cars were flying past us. The cars behind us we could barely see because the smoke was so thick and it was day time. I knew we would get pulled over by the first cop who seen us. So I pulled off onto a dirt road. It was a very narrow road with woods on both sides and no way to turn around. I drove for nearly a mile before we came to a house and realized it was not a road but a driveway. Lucky for us there was an area where we could turn around at. I didn't want to take a chance driving during the day with the car the way it was so we decided to stay on the road 'til night. We woke up with a .357 with the longest barrel I've ever seen pointing at us. The man holding it was the property owner and wanted to know what the hell we were doing on his land. We explained our situation and lucky for us he let us leave without any trouble.

"I stopped at a payphone and called my grandpa because he's been a mechanic for Coca-Cola and he knows about engines. After describing the problems he told me the engine was shot and something about the pistons and the oil pan. I know nothing about engines. He told me I could get this powder-type sealant stuff to mix with some oil and put in the oil tank to keep the car working for a while longer. Guess the problem occurred because I never once put oil in it the entire time I owned it. We drove to a mechanic shop and stole the stuff we needed. It seemed to have worked because the car stopped smoking. Still couldn't reverse or go fast.

"Finally in the backwoods of Alabama the damned thing just died as I was driving. We sat on the side of the road for about thirty minutes before a car drove past and actually came back to see if they could help. It was a man in his early thirties and his young wife who couldn't be no more than 18 if she was lucky. He said he had a tow truck and his own mechanic shop so he would be back with the tow truck. I let the man know we had no money to pay him for his help and he said we would work something out. We got in the car and let him tow us to his garage. When we got there, he looked at my car and told me the engine was shot. Pretty much the same shit my grandpa told me. I used the pay phone to call my mom who called my grandpa 3-way. I told him the situation and my grandpa said he would send me money Western Union for a bus ticket to come home. They couldn't afford a bus ticket for everyone to come home, so I turned the offer down. I told them I would keep them posted and see if we could figure something out. The guy that owned the mechanic shop said we could stay on his property in the car until we figured something out.

"Jonah figured we could sell them some of the stolen stuff we had so we showed them everything we had. We literally had a whole trunk full of cell phones, CD's, speed detectors, clothes, radios and much more. When we showed him everything the guy said he would sell us one of the vehicles he owned if we went out and stole some things for him. He made a list and we agreed to try to find everything he wanted. Jonah said we should bag up everything with serial numbers on it and get rid of it. So we put everything in garbage bags and asked if there was a lake or something nearby. The guy told us how to get to a creek nearby. We all walked to the creek and tossed them in when we got there. We stayed for awhile just swimming and having fun. When we got back Jonah and I decided to go out together to burglarize some houses to try to get the stuff on the guy's list so we could get a car from him. We walked off on our own for a few miles until we came upon a few shacks. The first place we checked no one was home and we walked right in through an unlocked door. Wasn't much of shit in the place. We got some jewelry, several bars of soap, and some other junk.

"We left and went back to the garage. We were hanging out there when I noticed two things. The guy was constantly flirting with Heidi and his wife was doing the same with Jonah. While hanging out, several police cars from Alabama and several more from Pensacola pulled into the lot we were on. I knew this was trouble, so I hurried up and called my mom on the payphone before any of the cops could get out of their vehicles. I let her know what was going on and that we had a gang of stolen stuff in the car. The police started talking to Heidi, Brad, and Jonah. They said they had some reports of kids breaking into vehicles and wanted to check my vehicle. None of them objected so the cops did their search. They said they were looking for a BB gun that was being used to break into car windows. Luckily for us, I popped out a panel in the trunk and hid the BB gun when we cleaned it out. The police asked who owned the CD's and Brad said he did. They tried catching him in a lie by asking him what CD's he had and all. Brad was on point and started running off a list. Then they found a planner book and asked who it belonged to. Heidi said it was hers. They tried catching her in a lie asking her what notes were written on what specific dates. She had been through the planner earlier when we cleaned out the car so she was on point. Then they found a leather woman's jacket that was for a big woman and asked who owned it. Jonah told them it was my mom's. While they kept searching, Heidi came over and told me everything that was going on. I was still on the payphone with my mom so I put her on point about the leather jacket.

"When the police got done they came to ask me about the stuff in my car. I told them exactly what everyone else did. They asked to speak to my mom and they confirmed the jacket being hers. They said we couldn't sleep in our vehicle and would have to find someplace else to stay. My mom said to get a ride to hotel and to call her from there and she would use her credit card to rent us a room. So the police left and the guy took us to a hotel about twenty miles away. Mom maxed out her credit card and got us a room for three nights. We were all excited to be there. It was a huge step up from sleeping in the car and showering outside with a hose. That was what we stole the bars of soap for. All of us would get naked at night, soap up and spray each other off. We also used the soap to wash our clothes. The first thing we all wanted to do was to take a real shower.

"When we went to the hotel, there was a bunch of old rednecks renting the room next to us. They were sitting around drinking and partying. While Heidi went in the shower first, we went to holler at the rednecks to see if we could sell them anything. They bought thirty dollars worth of shit. Heidi got done and went out by us. I went to take a shower and when I was done Brad, Jonah and Heidi all had beers. I asked for a beer and the damned rednecks told me I was too young. Shit had me .38 hot[10].

"I went to the liquor store and waited until someone came along and agreed to go in and buy me a bottle. I went back to the room and started slamming my bottle. Killed about half of it before I started sipping on it. Heidi came back to check on me with Jonah. They said they would bring me drinks, but I didn't want shit from nobody. Then Heidi said the rednecks wanted her to strip for them and they would pay her. She asked what I wanted her to do. I told them we wanted 400.00 dollars for the whole night. Once she spoke to me, the rednecks realized Heidi wasn't gonna do shit without my okay and that they should've given me a damned beer. They told Jonah to have me come over and drink with them and Heidi. I wasn't with that. Finally, they agreed to the price if the b-day redneck could fuck Heidi. Heidi is a down-ass bitch who will do what needs to be done, but she wouldn't do anything like that without me being down with it. I agreed and told Brad and Jonah to collect the money first and to make sure Heidi is safe. I wasn't about to go watch her strip and fuck no other men. These clowns were trying to give them like 70 dollars and tell them they would go to the bank the next day to get the rest. When Heidi told me that, I killed the whole idea and didn't even go back next door. Heidi and I ended up passing out in one bed and they shared the other.

"Next morning, Heidi and I were up first and one thing led to the next. Before we knew it, we were naked exploring each other's bodies. I had just mounted her and slid my dick into her pussy when the damned phone rang. It was the motel seeing if we wanted maid service. Of course, Jonah and Brad had to wake up. Heidi and I fooled around for a few minutes under the sheets after that but didn't have sex. Jonah called a friend of ours who is a mid-level Jamaican drug dealer and asked for his help. He agreed to Western Union us the money needed to buy a car. Then Jonah called the guy who had been letting us stay at his garage, and asked him to give us a ride to get the money. The guy picked us up and took us to his garage. He was trying to get work done on a car before we left.

"While he was working, his young wife asked us if we wanted to go to the store with her. She was trying to get away from her husband so she could mess around with Jonah. She said we would need to sneak off so her husband wouldn't know until after she was gone. She was driving down this dirt road when all of sudden her husband comes up behind us in his tow truck and smacks it against our bumper. The young wife was scared and wasn't gonna pull over. We talked her into pulling over. Her husband got her into his truck and towed us and the car back to his garage. When we got back, he told us to go down to the creek and he would pick us up to get the money. Before we left, Jonah sold him some stolen rings for ten dollars and some Oakley glasses.

"We started heading to the creek and before we made it there we decided to go back to the garage. On the way back there, a black lab puppy started following us from someone's yard. Jonah started calling it every time it started going back home. He said he was gonna keep it. I got pissed and said we had no damned food or shelter for our damned selves. How were we gonna take care of a dog? I walked ahead of them and when I got to the road where the garage was there was a bunch of cop cars. My friends caught up and were speculating what happened when a cop car spotted us. They whipped out of the parking lot and came flying towards us. We hauled ass and hid behind one of the only houses on the block. I was peeping around the corner the house when I looked back to say something all my friends were running into the woods. Only Heidi ran half way back for me and told me, "Let's go!"

"I thought running into the woods was a bad idea so I stayed put and let them run. I waited a minute until I thought the coast was clear; then I ran across the street in the other direction. A cop seen me running and came hauling ass out the parking lot after me. For some crazy reason, I tried running into the only other house on the block, but the door was locked. Before I turned around, I heard the cop telling me not to move and heard him cocking his shotgun. They put me in the car and kept asking me where my friends were. They had set up a boxed-in perimeter with K-9 dogs, so I knew my friends were doomed.

"As they drove around looking for them, I asked if I could yell out the window. I figured if they heard me yelling their alias names they would know to run the other way. The cops took me to this tiny little police station that only had one cell and was connected to the courthouse. I hadn't told them shit even though they kept asking.

"About ten minutes later, I seen them bringing in Heidi, Brad and Jonah. All of them had cuts and red welts from running through bamboo sticks and other sticks in the woods. Brad had lost his shoe in some mud. Heidi was soaked in water and mud 'cause she jumped into a pond trying to run from the police. She was by far the worst because she only had on a pair of Daisy Duke Shorts and a t-shirt on. The chief told me they had a witness who saw a black guy with a 'fro and a skinny white kid break into a house. He said they already knew it was Jonah but weren't sure if the other person was Brad or me. Finally, he said if we got back the rings none of us would be charged. He said the guy from the garage had called them about us 17 times over the past few days and gave them two of the rings already. This piece of shit had been acting like he was trying to help us the whole time, gave us a list of shit to steal for him, and come to find out he's the one calling the police on us. I told everyone to just tell the truth so we wouldn't be charged. Everyone did except for Jonah. He went saying he knows his rights and didn't do shit. They had let them use a hose to wash off and Jonah had thrown the rings in the garbage when they first got there. The police found the rings and told Jonah since he wouldn't cooperate he was being charged with burglary. They put Brad, Heidi and me into the empty courtroom. We were left alone with no cuffs on or nothing. They brought us each a soda and a meal from KFC. None of us could believe it. They didn't charge any of us.

"While in the courtroom, Heidi and I both knew we would be getting locked up for violating our probation. I tried talking her into having sex in the courtroom since we wouldn't be seeing each other again for a long while. She was in no mood though. She gave me all her jewelry and said she would get it all back when she got out. She was gonna have to do 5 years in a Wisconsin prison.

"None of us was 19, which was the legal age in Alabama, so they put us in a detention center for kids. When we got there, they told Heidi her probation officer would pick her up in a few days. They told me and Brad to call our parents and tell them they had to pick us up. Brad called his mom, and she said they were crazy. Police even got on the phone and told her she would be charged with child neglect if she didn't come pick him up. She just hung up on them. I called my mom and told her the situation. She was gonna leave that day for her vacation on the Mississippi River, so I told her just to enjoy her vacation and to pick me up after it was over. Of course, she said she would come get me first.

"They put all of us in separate dorms. The next day, we all went to school in the same class together. I wasn't trying to leave either of them so we plotted an escape. We found out certain days we got to go outside on rec. together and there was only a small fence holding us in. We were gonna jump the fence and haul ass. The day we were going to have rec., the guard threw my clothes into my cell and told me I was leaving. My parents were there to get me.

"At the front desk the guard was asking if they knew Brad and would they take him back to Wisconsin too. I couldn't believe my ears. My step-dad said he would need to speak to Brad first. They let him and I guess he wanted 100 dollars to take him. Brad would have agreed to anything. So they released Brad to us. I asked my parents to drive around the detention center and wait to see if Heidi came out for rec. I intended to have her jump the fence and come with us. We waited about 20 minutes, but nobody came out. My step-dad wouldn't wait no longer and I felt brokenhearted having to leave. Not only leaving Heidi but 'cause my homeboy Jonah was jammed up too. My parents drove back to the guy's garage so I could get some stuff from my car. When we got there, my mom managed talking the guy into buying the car for 150.00 dollars. We got the stuff out of the car and headed home."

HOUSE OF DETENTION

I hustled day-in and day-out to make sure I had everything I needed. I learned early on that when people get locked up their friends and family get that out of sight out of mind mentality. A person locked up can never fully depend on anyone but themselves to get by.

ANGEL MILES

"On the drive home the plan was to take Brad home and get the 100 dollars for my step-dad and they were gonna go on vacation. We went to Brad's house where we found out he got kicked out. So we all went to my mom's. I asked my mom if Brad could stay there since he had no place to live. She said yeah and she said she would get my step dad to agree. Then my mom says I could throw a birthday party at the house, which was in a few days, or we could come fishing with them for the week on the Mississippi River. Right away, I thought party. I told Brad and he said fishing. So that's what we did.

"We left that day for Buffalo City where my parents rented a cottage from a family right there on the river. My parents and James stayed at the cottage. The family friend Don let me use one of his boats and Brad and I decided to find a spot on the river to camp. We set up a tent right on a main channel on a sand island. Most of the days, we fished and swam. At night, we drove the boat around the piers where there were boat garages built right on the water. We broke into at least a dozen of them to search the big party boats inside. Most of the party boats would have liquor and beer in them. That night we stole about 30 bottles of liquor, fishing gear, gas tanks, a few cases of beer and some fireworks. We went back to our camp area and started drinking. We decided to make a fire, so we gathered all the wood we could find. It ended up being the biggest bon fire I've ever seen. We even drug huge fallen trees to put in the fire. I poured gasoline all over the wood. Flames had to have been at least 25 feet in the air.

"We started fishing off the shoreline and there were bushes and brush in our way. They were half on land and half in the water. So, I decided to pour gas on them and light them on fire so they wouldn't be in our way anymore. When I put fire to the gas, the fire started going down the river on top of the water. I didn't realize the gas would catch fire on the water, and it was a snake line of fire on the water going down at least 100 yards long. We were both very concerned someone would see it and call the DNR on us. Ain't no way we could put out the huge bon fire, the bush fire or the fire on the water. So, we just went back to drinking. About ten minutes later, the water fire went out. We passed out and when we woke up the next morning, the bush fire was almost out. Our bon fire was still going strong.

"We used the boat to get back to the cabin my family was at. My mom had got a number for a buddy of mine who lived in town named Tommy. He was a kid my age who I only seen when on vacation on the river. My mom gave me twenty dollars for my birthday and then they all went to go fishing. Tommy showed up not long after they left. My brother James stayed with Brad and I 'cause he wanted to see Tommy. Soon as Tommy arrived, I asked him if he could get a 20 sack of weed. I gave him the money and he gave it to the guy who drove him. Then Tommy handed me a sack that was about 2 and a half grams. Brad seen the sack and was ready to fuck up him and Tommy for trying us[11] like that. I knew Tommy was solid so I just let it go and told Brad to do the same. Tommy and his friend left.

"Brad, James and I went down to the pier to smoke. I rolled a pinner joint and we blazed. After hitting that pinner twice and passing it, I was already stoned out of my mind. When we got done we were all straight stuck on stupid. Brad was no longer feeling as if Tommy was getting over on us. That was some of the most fire[12] weed I ever blazed. We sat on the pier clowning for so long we never realized our parents were pulling into the pier. We all kind of panicked because James was stoned and mom was gonna be pissed. Mom and I knew Brad and I stay high, but it never stopped her from saying something. Brad and I just looked at each other and busted out laughing in tears. They pulled up and we helped tie the boat on the pier. Soon as my mom looked at us, she said, 'Damned dope heads found some dope even way out here I see.' Then she looked at James and said, 'I know you ain't getting your brother high.' I told her, "Of course not, but he was next to us when we smoked so he might have caught a contact."[13]

"She let it go at that. It was my birthday so Brad and I stayed at the cottage with my family that night. We all played cards for hours and drank coffee. Finally everyone went to sleep except for Brad and me. We were drinking cup after cup of coffee and using 4-5 big sugar cubes in each cup. Then we found a bottle of no-doze pills that are used to help keep you up. We split the bottle in half and each took like 18 pills. Both of us were so wired up, we got to thinking of other drugs. Somehow, the topic of 'shrooms growing on cow shit came up. I told Brad there was a cow pasture down the road. He said if we got there right as the sun was coming up there would be 'shrooms on all the cow shit that we could get. I was all for that. Having so much energy' we chose to walk instead of taking my parent's car. It was like 4 am when we left.

"About a mile into our journey, I rolled up a "pinner" and we blazed. After that joint, we both lost interest in our mission and we headed back to the cottage. When we arrived back at my parents, they were just getting up to go fishing. Brad and I had nothing else to do, so we took the boat out and went fishing too.

"The rest of that vacation Brad and I spent drunk and either fishing or swimming. When we got back to my mom's house after that vacation, we still had about 20 bottles of liquor left. I checked in with my probation officer by calling her. She wouldn't tell me whether or not she was going to "revocate" me, but I knew she was. She set a date for me to come see her, which was like twelve days from the day we spoke. Brad and I spent the whole first week back getting drunk and high with my friends, Jaime and Justin who lived down the street. I was so tore up that week I don't remember doing anything else. My main goal was to kill the remaining bottles of liquor before I had to see the probation officer. That didn't turn out to be a problem at all.

"I told Heather my situation and we spent a little time together. As always, we made up and pushed forward. The day I had to go in to see my probation officer, I had my mom drive me in. I knew once I stepped foot in her office, I was going to be locked up. Heather, James and Brad came along and I said goodbye in the parking lot. It was ironic; mom parked next to a van and I said that was the van that would be taking me to jail – only because it turned out to be true. I went into the building and checked in and as soon as I sat down, two police came in to get me. They cuffed me and took me out to the van to take me to the county jail. They did allow me to say goodbye to my people, at least.

"Booking at the Milwaukee county jail sucked. A person never knows how long they will get stuck in booking before they'll be processed and moved to a regular dorm. I've seen people get processed in a day and others it takes two weeks. The booking room has 3 TV's, 18 pay phones, several benches and 7 cells. There's a section for women that is separated by only a metal bar. You get fed these nasty-ass bologna sandwiches three times a day that have a solid hunk of butter on them. Hardly anyone eats them, unless they've been in booking for a few days. People use them as pillows. The benches are always packed. The cells are literally so full of people that you literally have to climb over people to use the toilets. It ain't no fun being stuck in a cell with a dozen other men and having to shit with them watching you. Ain't no place to sleep except the bench or the concrete floor.

"About the only fun in booking is getting some of the women to flash their tits, ass or pussy to us. Lucky for me, they processed me in only 2 days and moved me to a regular dorm. That same week, I went in front of the judge to be sentenced. He asked why I violated my probation by leaving the state. All I said was that I wanted to see the ocean. I was sentenced to 2, 9-month sentences running concurrently in the House of Corrections. They transferred me to HOC [House of Corrections] the same day. I was put in the annex building. It was an open dorm with about 60 bunks.

"For the most part, everything was laid back. I spent my days working out, playing cards for money and talking on the phone. I'd call my mom and have her, James or Brad 3-way call for me. My nights I used to write Heather, draw her things and listen to my radio walkman.

"Things went smooth for about three weeks. Then one day I call moms and Brad accepts the call. He's drunk as shit and he tells me he's gonna put enough money on my canteen so I won't need to go without anything the entire time I'm there. I told him, 'Don't be doing nothing stupid.'

"I call back the next day and James tells me Brad is in jail. His drunk ass broke into a place he used to work at called Allied Pools 'cause he knew the combination to the safe. It was just his luck, just five minutes before he got there, the Pick-n-Save next door was robbed. Police were looking for these people and wound up stumbling upon him doing crime. Around that same time, I ran into an Unknown named Oscar that I mentioned earlier. He remembered me as being one of the kids who use to throw bricks through his house windows. Once the word was out as to who I was, he had his buddies head-hunting for me. I was getting into fights, left and right. Most of the time I'd get called out and we'd take the fight into the bathroom so we could fight without getting caught and in trouble. These guys seen me as easy prey 'cause I was young and thin as a rail.

"After the third or fourth fight, they started approaching with more caution. I've always been a skinny guy, but I'm quick as hell, have long-ass arms and reach, can take a punch and have some of the hardest and boniest knuckles a person can have. One of the guys decided it best to take it to me in the day room where it was unexpected. He got in my face and I assumed we would take it to the bathroom next, but he swung on me right there. Got me with a good solid blow to my chin too. He must have thought the blow was gonna knock me out 'cause he didn't follow through with more. That was his mistake. I caught him with a three piece combo to the face, kneed him in the nuts, and then took him to the ground. We were tussling on the ground when the CO's pulled us apart. I got moved to the Hole and was mad as hell when my new Airmax shoes got stolen. I was in my shower slides[14] when the fight happened and my shoes were on my locker. Taught me a lesson though. I learned to keep my shoes on at all times.

"Although I had 9 months to do, I could have gotten released in 6 months with good time. So, being sent to The Hole meant more time I would be locked up. During my time, I got into some words with some dude. Each prisoner got to come out of his cell alone for one hour by themselves to shower and use cleaning supplies. This dude was mopping in front of my cell and slinging water all in my cell. I told the dude to watch where he's getting that nasty-ass water. Next thing I knew, he was at my cell with the mop and trying to use the stick to hit me through the bars. I just stood at the back of my cell where he couldn't reach me. The next day, early in the morning, I asked for my rec. time while everyone else was asleep. That same nasty-ass mop water was in the mop bucket. I rolled the bucket down to that dude's cell, picked it up and tossed it on him while he was sound asleep. He went screaming for the guards and told on me when they arrived. I got moved to another part of the

Hole.

"After I got off confinement and moved to a regular dorm, I found out through mom that Brad got moved to HOC. I had Heather come visit me and mom visit Brad so we could see each other. Brad was in a dorm where he could get cigarettes off the black market for cheap. So I would smuggle 20-30 candy bars with me to the visiting room to give him so he could get us tobacco. Back at my dorm I would sell each rolled up cigarette for three candy bars each.

"I got pretty tight with a black dude in my dorm named Greg. Dude was built and pretty much ran the dorm when it came to supplying contraband. He had plugs with several officers. We just clicked for some reason. We used to play as partners in Dominoes and Spades a lot, gambling with everyone in the dorm. It was very rare of us to lose at either game. We had other hustles too. He had a connection with someone in the kitchen to get 5-gallon bags of pure liquid coffee. Since I was a good thief, I would smuggle back to the dorm from the chow hall. One teaspoon of this stuff would make on strong cup of coffee. We would fill up 22 oz. tumbler cups and sell them at 5 dollars apiece. And, of course, he would get tobacco and weed to sell. Greg was cool and really fun to be around. He ended up being moved off the dorm.

"Shortly after that, I got into it with a new guy fresh on the wing. It really wasn't much of nothing though. I said something about the mail lady after she left our dorm after passing out the mail. This clown tells me to watch my mouth, speaking bad of her. Dude was about 6' 5" and 300 pounds. I was always taught that if you let anyone get away with messing with you, then everyone else would think they could do it. So although I didn't want any problems with this guy, I felt I had no other choice but to address him with violence. We were standing in the doorway of the TV room where the CO's couldn't see; I jumped in the air and punched the due in the face. Not wanting him to get his hands on me, I ran into the bunk area thinking I could buy some time 'cause he wouldn't do nothing in front of the CO's. Boy was I wrong. Dude chased me all around like a damned grizzly bear. The CO seen this and called for backup.

"We both went to confinement, but didn't stay there long because neither of us would tell them what happened. Lucky for me, I never seen that guy again. Brad ended up getting transferred to prison, so I never seen him again either. I got out of confinement and was surprised to be put in a dorm with someone I knew well from the streets … Jerry, my childhood girlfriend Haley's older brother was there. My first thought was to fight him because of how he ran off with my 200 dollars that time he was supposed to be getting me a QP of weed. He was so happy to see me; I just couldn't stay mad at him, especially since he told he was hooked on crack real bad at the time he did it. I knew him and his family way too long to stay mad at him over a little money. I asked about Haley and he said he was still in touch with her and we could call her. I had him call her right away. She was surprised and thrilled to be hearing from me. Even though we hadn't dated since before I was a teen. We were always good friends and the flirting just came back naturally for us both. We started talking on the phone and writing each other regularly. I was surprised to find out how she had 2 kids and lived only about eight blocks from Heather's.

"I remember the first time she came to visit me, I had finger waves in my hair. She smiled from ear to ear and said that's what she loved about me. I never cared what others thought and always did original shit. Ain't no white boy supposed to be having no finger waves, but I didn't give a fuck.

"I ended up getting a job in the kitchen and was moved to the kitchen worker dorm. I missed kicking it with Jerry, but I loved working in the kitchen. Every day I would sneak off with sheet pans of cookies, brownies, and cakes fresh out the oven and hide in one of the walk-in coolers. I'd sit in there for hours just chillin' and eating cookies and drinking milk. I got straight with another kitchen worker and he showed me the ropes. I learned how to make wine, which is called 'buck' or 'hooch' in prison. He showed me how to get tobacco, sneak stuff back to the dorm and sell them. The kitchen also had these big bags of Kool-Aid I would steal and sell.

"I was going to school and getting my HSED during that time also. It was very convenient because the class was mixed with people from other dorms, which made it possible for me to sneak stuff to people in other dorms to sell. I didn't really have people on the streets sending me money, but I never really needed anyone to. I hustled day-in and day-out to make sure I had everything I needed. I learned early on that when people get locked up their friends and family get that out-of-sight-out-of-mind mentality. A person locked up can never fully depend on anyone but themselves to get by.

"School was okay for the most part. I earned my HSED, which everyone on the streets told me would be useful to get a good job. When New Year rolled around, everyone in the kitchen was getting drunk. Guys were so openly drunk that CO's started doing random breathalyzer tests. Plenty of guys got knocked off that day and went off on confinement. I lucked out and was given a breathalyzer before I started drinking.

"I was due to be released on the day of Heather and my anniversary on January 15th, so I started to settle down. I wanted more than anything to get out and be home with her for our anniversary. I avoided a lot of bullshit to avoid confinement.

About a week before the 15th I was sitting in the chow hall eating when a guy at my table started arguing with me. He jumped up, spilling his milk and creating a scene. The milk was flowing off the table so I jumped up to avoid it getting on me. The CO assumed we were gonna fight and took us both to confinement. That extended my sentence by ten days which meant I didn't make it home for my anniversary with Heather."

CRACKING UP

ANGEL MILES

"Shortly after that incident, I was released. My parents and brother and brother were living with my cousin John at his home on 74th and Lisbon. The house was really full 'cause my grandma, cousin Toya, Shawn and cousin Mary also lived there. Also my cousin's boyfriend Goldie lived there too. Since I got out shortly after X-mas my parents left the tree up and had some presents out for me. We had a X-mas party the day I got out. It was a great feeling, seeing my family do that for me.

"I went back to living with Heather. People think that being locked up is a way for criminals to be rehabilitated and become productive members of society, but the system only teaches them new crimes and how to be better criminals. I didn't waste any time going back to my street life and hustling ways I knew. It was only a matter of days before I decided to holler at Haley. I called her up one night and told her I wanted to stop by. It was pretty late, and she told me to go to her bedroom window because her dad was sleeping.

"When I got there, she had me climb through the

window. She shared a room with her mom and 2 kids. That was the first time I ever seen her kids but they were sleeping. I spent some time talking with Haley and her mom catching up. Haley and I ended up having sex for the first time that night. Neither of us was concerned with her mom or the kids being in the same room or anyone waking up.

"After that night, I spent time at her house frequently. She was a few months pregnant, but that didn't matter none to me. I was still hanging with Jason and that crowd all the time. Jason's sister Valerie was smoking hot and every guy she encountered tried to get in her pants. No doubt, I wanted to also but my swag[15] was too much to show it. I never let on that I wanted it. In fact, I did just the opposite and acted as if her beauty had no effect on me. When a person is used to being pursued and having their pick of choice, they tend to be attracted to a challenge, the ones who are forbidden or who show no interest. It didn't take long.

"One night, we were at her house and everyone else had left. It wasn't unusual for me to crash at her house on the couch. We were friends and enjoyed each other's company. She asked if I wanted to play some cards. I jokingly said, "Yeah if it's strip poker." To my surprise, she agreed. Poker's my game, so I knew she would be naked way before me. I didn't want her being naked alone, so I started losing on purpose once she was down to her panties and bra. She made a comment about her titties not being much to look at 'cause they were so small. This insecurity of hers came as a shock to me. When she took her bra off, I sure wasn't complaining. After we were both ass naked, I knew she was expecting me to make a move on her, so I did just the opposite and said "good game" and started getting dressed. I could see this only made her want me more and that was my intention, but not just for that night. The next night we ended up having sex for the first time. I knew the more I avoided her and acted like l was sleeping with her was no big deal, the more she would chase me trying to prove me wrong.

"I did a lot of bouncing around from place to place for a

while. Some days, I would spend with Haley at her place. Some days, I would spend with Valerie. Other days, I would spend with Heather and Austin or with my family. I tried to stay away from my family a lot because I knew I was a bad influence on my brother and my cousins. One time, I stayed with my family and my cousin Shawn and my brother James decided to find a house to break into. Nobody was home, so I busted the lock and we robbed the place for everything we could carry out. There was never no telling what kind of stupid shit we would do when we got together.

"Another time, James and I went to a gun show with my step-dad and my grandpa. I ended up having James distract one of the gun dealers while I stole a .45 police-edition pistol from the dealer's display. I walked right out of the building and took the gun to my grandpa's van. I couldn't believe how easy it was to steal. James kept trying to get me to go back inside to steal one for him, but there was no way in Hell I was gonna give him a gun even if I could steal another one. I never did go back inside.

"About a week later, I drove over to see the family again. I wanted to go to the store about two blocks away and didn't want to use the car. James and Shawn were gonna ride their bikes, so I jumped on one of the younger cousin's bikes. It was a little old raggedy-ass bike with a banana seat. I didn't give a damn though. On the way to the store, we rode passed a group of kids about my age or so who mugged[16] us the whole time we passed. So on the way back I told James and Shawn to ride on ahead of me a few yards when we passed the group. We were on a main street with heavy traffic so I didn't expect no trouble. I had that .45 on me so I didn't expect no trouble, either. I passed the group of kids and they were acting in a manner as if they were debating on fucking with me or not. I stopped a few houses down the block, got off the bike and acted as if I was fixing the chain. Next thing I see is 2 of the dudes walking up on me. They started talking shit about me and the bike and I told them to get lost. James and Shawn rolled back up by me and these clowns said they would beat all our asses if we don't get off their block.

"One dude walked up on me and I decked his ass so hard he hit the ground and was in no rush to get back up. I was ready to take on his buddy until I saw about a dozen more come out the house running towards us. I know James and Shawn are soldiers and would have stood with me against the odds, but I didn't want to tussle having a loaded gun in my pants. We got on the bikes and hauled ass home. These clowns wouldn't let it go and chased us. I upped that .45 and pointed it at them as I was riding and they all turned tail fast. That was the only time I ever tried pulling my gun without using it. I wound up getting this job at a telemarketing place and sold that gun to a guy who worked there for 225 dollars. Only sold it 'cause I lost my job.

"My cousin Toya's boyfriend Goldie told me he had this house to do a home invasion on. The place is a big-time drug house he used to once live in and worked out of for the people. I was supposed to be going to work, but let him talk me into skipping work to rob these drug dealers. Come to find out that him and his buddies didn't have any working guns. One of them had a broke-down 30-30 rifle that didn't even have the lever or trigger to it. They tell me the people in this house only keep one gun. I ain't happy, but I'm still down because of the money involved. We spent several hours planning everything. When we got started, they all started arguing about who was gonna carry the gun. My gun! That's when I knew we had a problem. Each one of them wanted to carry my gun and I wasn't gonna part with it. I knew I'd shoot those dealers with no hesitation, but I didn't know if Goldie or his buddies would. That ended that plan as well as my job telemarketing.

"A little bit after that, Mom was in the neighborhood and decided to pick me up from Heather's to take me out to eat with the family. I happened to run into Casey and she said her and some friends were having a party at some hotel. She asked if I wanted to stay the night at the hotel. Although I knew from past experience that she was a bad lay, I figured I'd check the party out just because. I asked mom if I could use the van for the night because I didn't want Heather trippin' about the car. Mom said it wasn't a problem. So I agreed to meet Casey at the hotel. I asked if there would be any weed there, and she said she didn't know. She left and I had mom stop at the neighborhood liquor store so I could pick up some bottles for the party. As I came out of the liquor store, I noticed my Jamaican homeboy's Eddie Bauer truck at the gas station across the street. He was my next stop anyway, so I ran across the street to holler at him. Picked up an ounce of weed from him and two boxes of blunts at the store before leaving; dropped the family off at their house and went straight to the hotel.

"When I walked in, I knew I was the party. There was no alcohol or drugs except what I brought. It was two females and four dudes just sitting around. I was already committed, so I tried making the best of the situation. I had 7 bottles of liquor and an ounce of weed, which I was determined to drink and smoke up all of that night. None of the dudes smoked weed and one of them didn't even drink. I rolled up 10 blunts, and then started pouring drinks for everyone. The girls and I smoked blunt after blunt while drinking. I was drinking about four cups of alcohol to everyone else's one, except for Casey. She tried to keep up with me.

"After about four blunts were gone, I realized Casey was missing. She had went into the bathroom and passed out on the floor after puking in the toilet. I just left her laying there on the floor and went back to doing my thing. Two of the dudes passed out so it was just a sober dude, me and a chick hanging out. Her and I kept blazing until she couldn't smoke no more. She was smoked out. Nobody else was drinking, so I just started slamming gulps from each bottle. I blazed a blunt by myself and kept drinking. The other 2 were dozing off by the time I finished my blunt.

"There was one blunt left, so I blazed it and tried to get the chick to smoke it with me. She hit it once and when I went to pass it back to her she was passed out.   Last thing I remember is lying on the floor, smoking my blunt. Next thing I knew I was laying face down on the bed being woke up by the cops. I had only been asleep about 2 and a half to three hours so I was still tore up. They had already searched me and found a weed pipe and 2 grams of weed. One of the cops was dumping out the liquor bottles in the bathroom. Everyone else was standing up against the wall. I was in no mood for bullshit. So when the cop told me I better tell him who I got the weed from I told him, to go suck a dick 'cause I ain't telling him shit. People from the "party" were telling them I brought the weed and the alcohol. The cops drug me into the hallway and slammed me into the wall; started threatening me with years in prison if I didn't say who I got the weed from. I just laughed and told them to take me to jail because I would be out before the day's over. They only got me with a weed pipe and at most a dime bag of weed. I knew all they could do was give me a ticket and release me for that shit.

"They took me to the jail and booked me. When they emptied my pockets, I had maybe a gram's worth of loose weed that must have fallen from the bag. The cop emptied it along with the lint onto the counter and said that would be another charge. He turned his back and I got a baggie and licked up the weed and the lint off the counter. That cop was so mad that I still laugh when I think about it; probably didn't help when he said I would be charged with the weed and I said, "What weed?"

"I was released a few hours later with a few tickets; had someone pick me up and take me back to the hotel to pick up mom's van; dropped her van off at the house. I never seen or messed with Casey after that.

"I started spending a lot more time at Heather's with her and our son. Heather worked a lot so when she worked I brought Austin over to Valerie's so he could play with the other kids. It allowed me time to spend with Val also. Things were going pretty good between Heather and I for a while. That never lasted too long for us though. Heather and I started verbally fighting. I don't recall what it was about.

"She was cussing me out and someone rang our doorbell. I answered the door and to my surprise it was my cuz Paul standing there. It had been a long while since I seen him.

Heather was still bitching and I was tired of hearing her shit. Soon as I seen my cuz, he tried to embrace me with a huge hug, but I walked right past him and jumped in his car. There were already two people in his car, which I later found out were his roommates named Shorty and Mariah. Paul got in the car and asked me what was up. I told him the usual bullshit and that I'd be crashing with him that night. Of course, he had no problem with that and said I could stay at his place as long as I'd like. Since the last time I had seen him, he had come up in the world. Had his own place, which was a nice 2-bedroom apartment in Saukville. He shared it with a guy named Shorty, Mariah and his wife. I was surprised Paul went and got himself married. He had a nice-ass Cadillac with a banging system. Things were going good for him.

"When we got to his house, he introduced me to his wife, Lisa, and let everyone know I had the run of the house and I would be staying a while. Nobody had a problem with that at first but that changed after me being there a while. Paul is like me in many ways. That was good for me but bad for everyone else. What I thought would be only a few days hanging with my cuz turned out to be a few months. We always got along so well and enjoyed being around each other. The first day or two, we mostly did a lot of catching up. Like me, Paul was always one who didn't like to sit still for too long and loved to be driving around. Although it was his Cadillac, he did not drive 'cause he had no license, so he would have Mariah driving. Cuz was a damned fool! He always acted as if he was a Don or something. The crazy thing is people in his circle treated him like he was. Nobody went against what Paul wanted or said. That always caused conflict because in Paul's eyes I could never do no wrong. So if anyone ever voiced a complaint towards me, or expected him to side with them against me, they were in for a rude awakening.

"Shorty and I got along well because he smoked weed and was a thief like me. Mariah was a good-looking female that just wanted to have fun. Lisa was Paul's wife so I tried to get along with her just for that reason. After a few days at Paul's house, I knew I would be there for a while. I was wearing his shoes and clothes, which was okay but I wanted my own stuff. So I told cuz we needed to go to Milwaukee while Heather was working so I could pick up some stuff.

"When we got to Heather's, I packed up enough stuff for several weeks. On the way back to his house, we stopped at Wal-mart. While we were there, I stole a BB gun and a gang of other shit. When we got back to the car, I started pulling out all the shit and everyone was shocked. None of them had ever seen me take anything. That opened the door for a several-week crime spree. We started driving around to every store just to steal. Paul wasn't much down with stealing much himself, but Shorty, Mariah and I were. None of them was on my level of stealing so I showed them a few tricks of the trade. For weeks all we did is drive all over to steal. We had so many paintball guns and BB guns it was ridiculous. Every night we would steal bottles of liquor and get drunk. Lisa didn't really drink and hated when Paul did. She never came stealing with us either and hated when Paul went with us.

"Paul loved to get systems and other stuff for his car. I remember we went to this audio system store because he wanted to buy a newer model CD deck for his ride. I walked in and there was a box with 2 twelve-inch speakers in a box he was looking at. I asked if he wanted them. He said he already had 2 15's in his trunk, but that he wouldn't mind adding the box with the 12's as well. I told him to go get his new CD deck and I'd meet him in the car. I picked that box up and walked right out of the store. When he got back from the store, he seen a coat draped over the box and he just laughed. He couldn't believe I actually stole it. Ain't nothing I wouldn't have done for my fam. And, I must say, them extra subs had his system hitting it so hard it shook foundations.

"One day Shorty and I were on the couch smoking a joint when I grabbed one of the BB guns. We had a gang of BB guns lying all over the place. I took a BB gun outside and put a weed seed in the barrel then I put it back on the table. After we got done smoking I picked up a BB gun and put the barrel against the bottom of Shorty's bare foot. I told him to say "I won't." and this fool said it, so I shot him. Dude jumped screaming so fast and leaking blood everywhere, I couldn't do shit but laugh. He picked up a BB gun and started busting at me. Next thing I knew we were running through the house having an all-out BB gun war. Paul heard all the commotion, and when he seen us, he picked up a BB gun and started shooting at Shorty and telling him he better chill. Things settled down quick. Turns out I grabbed the wrong gun and shot Shorty in the foot with a BB. That thing was so deep inside his foot we couldn't even see it. Paul being the fool he is decided he would perform "surgery" to fix it. He had me laughing so hard I was in tears. He went into the bedroom and came out wearing rubber gloves, a doctor's mask and carrying tools he needed. Took him about 20 minutes before he finally got the BB out. Every time Shorty started screaming out or jerking his foot up, Paul grabbed the BB gun and told him he would shoot him again and they would have to start the whole process again. We were always doing some fun shit like that. A lot of nights we would gear up and go on a big field trip for paintball fights. We would drive right onto the field and cut on the lights so we could see. Usually it turned out Paul and I teaming up against Shorty. We never had any more BB gun wars in the house. Lisa wasn't too happy with us for all the Bb holes we put in the walls and all the shit we broke.

"One day, Paul wanted to go somewhere. Mariah said she was tired of driving. Paul started putting her in her place, but I stepped in and said I'd drive. He asked me if I had my license and I lied, saying I did. From that point on I did all the driving. Mariah didn't mind at first, but she did mind when Paul removed her part of the back seat so the system would hit harder. People sitting in the back had to rest their backs against the metal frame. Paul was hooked on pain killers called oxycodon. His supplier stayed in Milwaukee. So we were constantly driving there. The first time we stopped there he bought some 80 milligram pills and he offered me one. I never tried one, so I told him to give me a quarter of one for starters so I could see how it is. He popped one and I took a quarter.

"His grandparents stayed in Milwaukee so he decided to visit. I hadn't seen them in years. Soon as we arrived I sat down on the couch and that couch started hitting me hard. I told Paul and he said to go wait out in the car. He came out a minute later. I started pulling out of the driveway and that moment I slammed on the brakes, opened the door and puked my guts out. I told Mariah she had to drive. I never took that shit again.

"Another time, we were leaving Paul's supplier and we decided to stop at this sporting goods store. This sexy black chick working there seen us pull up. While we were in the store, I noticed the woman and told cuz I wanted to get her number before we left. This fool calls her over to us right then and says, "My cuz thinks you're sexy as hell and wanted to holler at you." We started to talk and I asked if she needed a ride home when she got off work. I gave her my cell phone number and told her to Holler. Later that night, she gave me a call. Paul, Shorty and I gave her a ride home. Turns out she only lived about a half mile away from where she worked. We hung at her place for a while. I was mainly interested in what kind of plug I could get from her at her store, though. When I brought the issue up, she said she was down for whatever. I said we would come to her register with a bunch of stuff and she would only charge us for the cheapest item.

"So the next day while she was working, we went to her job. Paul and I took several hundreds of dollars worth of items and only paid for socks. It became a routine for us to do a few times a week. Afterwards, we would take her home and chill at her house. During this time, she would pull me off into her room and try to get me to fuck, but I wasn't with it. She was a pretty girl who I would have slept with. My problem was the condition of her house. She lived in the projects, but that is no excuse to let the inside of your house look like a dump. It's a huge turn off for me. My logic is if a woman can't keep her house clean then she sure as hell isn't keeping her body clean. My cuz already knew what the deal was, so he would give me enough time to fool around before he would interrupt and say we had to bounce.

"Everything was going fine for a while. One night after leaving her house, we were pretty fucked up and stopped at a gas station because we had the munchies. I left the keys in the ignition with the car running. We went inside and got nachos, hot dogs and a gang of snacks. We were eating the stuff while waiting in line. When it was time to pay, I realized I had left my wallet in the car. Paul and Shorty waited in the store while I went to the car. Unknown to me whenever the doors open and close, it automatically locks the doors. So, I had locked the keys in the car. The store clerk thought we were trying to rob him, so he called the cops. None of us wanted to wait around to see them, so Paul smashed the small side rear window and we hauled ass out of there. The next day the chick from the sporting goods store wanted us to come by and get her a three-hundred-dollar tent along with anything else we were going to get. She also wanted me to give her 150 dollars cash. I had no problem with that.

"We went to the store and got her the tent as well as a bunch of stuff to give my family. After we dropped the stuff off, we were headed back to pick the chick up from work. A few blocks from the store, Shorty started having a breathing attack and didn't have his inhaler. I wanted to stop at the chick's work to let her know what was up, but the drive home was already gonna be 45 minutes. And Shorty said he couldn't waste no more time. As I was driving back to the house she called me asking where I was. She said I played her 'cause she hadn't got the money or the tent. She went off on me and hung up. I felt shitty about it but there wasn't much I could do.

"That put an end to that plug; a few days later, Shorty and I were chillin' at the house when Paul, Lisa and Mariah came home all excited. Shorty was on his way out the door to go to work. Soon as he left, Paul told me they had broken into someone's house. It was an ex-friend of Lisa's and she knew they would be on vacation. I asked them what they all got and they told me the garage was attached to the house and they only took stuff from the garage. When I heard this I said I wanted to go back with them and go into the house this time. Everyone was down with that so they took me to the house.

"I wasn't expecting what I seen when they pulled up the driveway. This house was secluded by woods and it was huge. When we got into the garage, I immediately kicked in the door leading into the house. Once we were in the house, we all went our separate ways. I knew these people were wealthy when I seen a full-sized slot machine in the first room I entered. There must have been thirty dollars in quarters just sitting inside the cash slot. There was this huge gun cabinet showing these collector rifles with gold all on them. Inside the drawers were handguns. I checked out the other rooms to check what the inventory was before I started taking stuff. It seemed everyone else was targeting the main bedroom and had already started taking stuff. To my surprise they weren't taking things I knew to be of the most value. The girls were taking clothes, trinkets and other little things. Paul was getting jewelry.

"I noticed everyone was at the car waiting on me. I saw a nice-sized safe in the walk-in closet and told them that's what we need to take. They said to leave it 'cause it only had paperwork inside it. Ain't no way I was gonna believe these people didn't have money in that safe nor was I gonna leave it. I tried getting it myself and was struggling with it. So I talked Paul into helping me. We dragged it out to the car. When we went back inside, it was like they all started panicking and wanted to leave. I noticed a door I hadn't checked so I checked it. When I opened the door it led to the basement. I went downstairs and I was blown away by all the rifles and shotguns I was seeing. A lot of them still had price tags on them. I grabbed several of them, taking them to the car. Everyone was at the car waiting on me. I was gonna go back in and get more stuff but everyone was ready to leave and said they would leave me if I did. I didn't understand the rush since the family wouldn't be home for two weeks. We could have easily gotten $80,000 worth of stuff from the house. Paul was in the process of moving and already had the keys to his new place so we went there since the place was empty. We took everything upstairs. To my surprise Paul had taken some of the handguns I had wanted to get. There was a real nice long-barrel .357 I had wanted and a four-barrel .22 Derringer I really wanted. He also had some expensive jewelry. Mariah had a jug of change, some clothes and a radio. Lisa only had clothes that I knew about.

"My mind was on getting the safe opened. Paul and I spent over 30 minutes with hammers and screwdrivers trying to pry it open. Nobody thought there was money inside but me. When we finally opened it up, we dumped everything out. When everyone saw all that money hitting the floor they dove right at it. I had to push everyone away and calm them down. While doing so I cuffed a handful of hundred dollar bills that were inside one of them bank wraps the banks use to bundle money. After all was calm, we started splitting up the money. Each of us was designated to split up different denominations among the group. I took all the twenty dollar bills to divide. Paul had the 100's, Lisa the 50's, and Mariah the 10's, 5's and 1's. As we were each making our own four piles with the money we were dividing, I noticed money was being cuffed. I chose to split the 20's because there were way more of those than any other. As I split the money into piles everyone else was finishing up, giving the piles they split, and taking three piles of what the others split. I had four piles of 20's I was still splitting when they took their piles. I still had a pile of 20's in my hand about 2 inches thick that they didn't give me a chance to divide. I just placed it on top of the money they gave me. I hurried up and put all the money in my pockets.

"Then someone says we should all count our money to make sure it was all split up evenly. I said I was happy with whatever I had and wasn't counting my money. Mariah said she had about 920. Paul said he had about 1,700. Lisa said she had like 1300. I never said shit. I wanted some of the handguns and liked the fat-ass ruby necklace they got. He offered to sell me the guns and the necklace for like 500. It was a great price, but I wasn't about to pay for shit. I felt like I was the one who stole the safe when no one else wanted to. I shared all that money with everyone, so they should have shared the shit they stole with me. I was pissed but didn't say anything. I told them I wanted a ride to Jason's and we needed to get rid of the safe. We drove to the Milwaukee River, dumped the safe over the bridge, and then went to Jason's. They dropped me off and I stayed with Valerie that night. Paul ended up picking me up the next day to go back to his apartment.

"That night we were all getting wasted when Lisa started getting slick out of her mouth with me. I was pretty drunk and in no mood for her shit. Then she gets into it with Shorty and I both. At that point I told Shorty, "Let's just leave." So we left in the middle of the night with no place to go. We walked aimlessly for about an hour before we decided to steal a car and go to Milwaukee. The first car we were gonna steal had an alarm. We went a block further and came across a car parked in a driveway next to a barn. The door was unlocked. So we both got in. As I was about to pop the column, Shorty noticed a key lying in the console between the seats. To our surprise it was the key for the ignition. I put the car in neutral and let Shorty push it to the road before I started it.

"When we got to Milwaukee, we were still drunk, had no place to go and decided to go on a crime spree. We robbed so many cars that night we had no room left in the car to fit anything more. I decided to rent a hotel room to store everything. We unloaded the car and went back out stealing. One of the vans I broke into I found a wallet belonging to some guy named Daniel Dawson. It had a debit card along with several other credit cards. Shorty hit a car which he found a wallet that had 2 credit cards in it. After two nights of non-stop breaking into vehicles, we had shit piled up to the ceiling at the hotel. We had more speaker boxes, speakers, amps, CD's and CD decks than we knew what to do with. We got bored with that and decided to go shopping with the stolen credit cards. We hit every mall and store possible to use the credit cards. Wound up running into Paul, Lisa and Mariah at one of the malls. After using the cards so much the ones Shorty had wouldn't work no more. We were in a Footlocker and had about 700 dollars worth of shoes and clothes and tried putting it on the card when we found out it wasn't good no more. I didn't want to draw any attention to us so I wound up just paying cash.

"After that, I went off alone with my little brother James who was with us. I stopped at a jewelry store and dropped almost 1,700 dollars on a nice gold chain with a panther charm that had ruby red eyes and diamonds in it. Then James and I hit up the leather store and I picked up a leather Pelle Pelle jacket that was all black with a huge panther on the back of it for 400 dollars. I tried getting James to pick out a jacket for himself but he didn't want me spending all that money on him. I wasn't concerned about no money, but he still refused. I wish I would have just picked one out for him, but I didn't. We hit a few more clothes stores where I picked up a few more Pelle Pelle, Shawn John and Avirex outfits as well as some Pelle Pelle hats. After that, we went back to the shoe store where I bought a different pair of shoes for each of those outfits. Shorty, James and I left the mall and dropped James off at home before going back to the hotel. Shorty called Mariah to come by and pick him up.

"Paul wanted me to go with him to check out a truck he was interested in buying. So we drove to Saukville to look at this truck. The guy wanted 1,500 dollars and the damn truck didn't have anything in it. It literally didn't have any seats, any of the interior at all or even tail lights. It was a nice-ass truck with a fresh money-green paint job, but would take several more thousand to fix it up. Paul's crazy ass lets the guy talk him into paying 500 cash for the truck and giving him his Cadillac also. Had I known Paul was gonna do that dumb ass shit, I would have just bought Paul's Cadillac for a 1,000 dollars. That guy sold Paul's Cadillac the same week for 5,500 dollars.

"We left with the truck and hit up several junk yards to buy seats and other shit needed for the truck. Mariah used her parent's car to take me back to Milwaukee. We stopped at a liquor store about three blocks from the Northridge mall to get some cigarettes. When I went in I ran into the black chick I was getting the plug from at the sporting goods store. She was .38 hot 'cause I beat her out of the money. I just ignored her and she left. When I walked out the store, I heard the sound of breaking glass. When I turned around to see what it was this bitch wanted, she had snatched the chains off my neck and had a broken bottle to my throat. The store clerk came out and said he was calling the cops on me. She ran off and jumped into her friend's car. I wanted to go after her, but I kept thinking of the stolen credit cards on me and the police coming. More than anything, I wanted to explain to her that I didn't intentionally hurt her or beat her out of anything. Instead, we jumped in the car and we left. I wasn't all that mad that she'd robbed me of almost 2,000 dollars worth of jewelry 'cause I'd have done the same thing in her shoes. I was mad because one of the chains and charms was a graduation gift from my grandpa. I was even more pissed that these clowns I was with didn't even attempt to help me when the shit went down.

"I cussed them out the whole drive to Jason's. They dropped me off and left. I had a feeling they were going to the hotel to get the shit Shorty and I had there, so I told Jason to give me a ride there. When we pulled up, Shorty was just getting into Mariah's car. He said he just picked up his clothes and he didn't want none of the other shit. They left and Jason and I went to my room. Come to find out Shorty took all the electronics Shorty and I bought using the credit cards. I didn't care though. We packed as much as we could into Jason's car and just left the rest there for the hotel to deal with. I decided it wouldn't be a good idea to leave the stolen car in the hotel parking lot and wound up filling up that car too. We still left enough stereo equipment there to supply a small store. We dropped everything off at Jason's and then he followed me to abandon the car. I had him drop me off at my mom's. I asked mom to use her van so I could go get Paul's and my stuff.

"When I got to Paul's apartment Shorty was there. Paul

had moved some of my stuff to his new place already. I didn't know how to get there so Shorty came with me. When we got to Paul's new place I loaded the van with my stuff. I don't know where the thought came from, but when we were leaving I decided to break into the bar below Paul's new apartment. So with no hesitation that's what Shorty and I did. We stole several boxes of all kinds of different liquors. I dropped him off back at the other apartment and drove back to mom's house, gave mom a few bottles, left my clothes and had Jason come pick me up. I spent several days at Val's partying non-stop.

"I was mad I lost my chains so I went to the mall and bought something bigger and better than the last one I had. Ended up getting another panther chain and charm that was only a few hundred more than the one I lost. A few days later, I ran into a guy who stayed a few blocks from Val's. He operated an ice cream truck. I seen an opportunity to get rid of some of the stolen amps, speakers and CD decks I had. I told him to let me fill up his truck and, while he sold ice cream, I would sell and give him a cut. So that's what we did. I made about 700 dollars that day. Then he tells me he knows a guy who might want to buy some stuff. We stop at the dude's house and we go in. When he comes back out he says dude wasn't home. Next thing I know, we're in an alley and stopped. He pulls out a crack pipe and puts a dime of crack in it. Then he says for me to smoke it with him. Shit caught me off guard because I never fucked with crack and didn't know he did. I told him crack was for crack heads and I wasn't doing it. He asked how I can knock something if I never tried it. So I smoked it with him. I didn't feel high when we were done.

"Later that night, he says I should go with him to this bar. I was only 17 and asked if he was sure he could get me in. He said, "Yeah," so I went. We get there and I start drinking and playing pool. After maybe an hour, I was wasted and buying everyone in the place drinks. Next thing I know I'm in a car with two dudes and the dude is taking me to buy crack. I figured what the hell and bought a 100-dollar piece. We smoked that up quick and I bought another 100-dollar piece. I was so damned high, but felt like I needed to smoke more. We smoked that up and I bought another 200-dollar piece which was all they had left. After smoking all that we went back to the bar and drank until closing.

"The same people we got crack from were the people giving us a ride. We stopped at a gas station and I went to use the pay phone 'cause someone paged me and my cell was dead. While I was on the phone, three cars full of dudes pulled into the gas station. I got off the phone and started walking back to the car. A guy from one of the cars that just pulled in was walking towards me. I tried to avoid walking into him and this clown still bumps into me. I turned around and dude tells me I ain't no gangsta and to turn my hat straight. I tell him I ain't turning shit straight, and if he don't like it he can turn it straight for me. Dude knocks my hat off and before I even know it I am surrounded by his buddies. I picked up my hat and was about to get in the car when one of the dude's buddies ran up on me with a gun and snatched my chain off my neck. I ain't no fool and wasn't gonna make no deal out of it. Material shit can be replaced but my life can't. I tried getting in the car when another dude starts to kick the door closed. He starts pulling at my jacket and telling me to come up out of it. Now it's one thing for someone to snatch something off me before I can stop it, and a whole different story to let someone make them give me my shit. It just wasn't gonna happen. I folded my arms and told them they would have to kill me to get my jacket. Lucky for me they weren't no real killers. They jumped in their car and hauled ass.

"All I wanted to do was to get to Val's and put the day behind me, but the clown I was with had other plans. He says he's gonna cheer me up and we get dropped off at some chick's house. He tells this chick to please me any way I want. She's asking if I want some pussy or some head, and I'm telling them they both lost their damn minds. I was wasted; I just got robbed; and I wanted to get back to Val's. Then dude hands me the charm from the chain I got robbed for; says it was lying on the ground and he was thinking about not even telling me. I was so pissed; I crushed the charm in my hand and threw the pieces on the floor. I left and walked until I found a pay phone. I called mom and she started going off saying she wasn't getting up at no 3:30 am to come get me. I lost my cool. I told her I just got robbed. I was wasted; I didn't know where the hell I was and she started complaining again about why I didn't call Heather or a friend. I told her, "Fuck you!" and hung up.

"I sat there for about 5 minutes trying to sober up and get my thoughts together. Then I started walking. I walked for about 6 blocks before realizing where the hell I was. Turned out I was only about one mile from Val's house. As I was walking mom pulled up. I was so mad I refused to let her give me a ride and kept walking. She followed me for several blocks before I ran through some yards to ditch her. I finally got to the house just as the sun was coming up. I didn't have a key or the door code to get in. Val always kept a window unlocked so I could climb to the roof and go through a window if needed. I was still messed up in no mood to climb so I just sat on the porch. The dogs woke Jason up and he came out. I told him what happened. We smoked a blunt and then I went upstairs to Val's and crashed. After that night I vowed two things. I'd never use crack again, and I would never get caught slippin' without a gun again.

"I was pretty much broke at this point, but I managed to get my hands on a little .380 chrome hand gun with the money I had left. I kept it on me at all times. Heather told me the police had been looking for me. So I stayed away from home. Valerie and I spent a lot of time together and fell in love. We kept our relationship secret though, at least for a while. One night we went to a pool party and her best friend Andrea was gonna stay the night at Val's for the after party. We got to Val's house and I was to sleep on one couch and Andrea on the other. Val went to her room to go to sleep. I was lying on the couch and Andrea sat by me and asked if I'm asleep. I told her not yet. She asked me if I wanted to fuck. My first thought was that sure would teach Val a lesson for leaving me out here on the couch when I should be in bed with her. I was in love though and wasn't gonna do nothing to hurt her. I told Andrea some lame excuse. Then she says, "Well at least let me suck your dick." All I kept thinking about was why she had to spend the night and why I wasn't in bed with Val making love.

"After several rejections she finally got the point and was not happy with me at all. I told Val about it the next day and she didn't know whether to believe me or not. After that I didn't go out my way to hide our relationship.

"My family was going on vacation to the Mississippi river and asked me if I wanted to join them. I asked if they minded me bringing Valerie and her daughter Latecia. Of course, they didn't mind. I talked Val into going with me. I had heard dude down the street had set me up to get robbed when I did crack with him. I also knew he started selling weed and just got a QP from a buddy of mine. I needed money so I went to his house when he was at work and kicked in the door. I found the weed and that was the only thing I took. I called some people up and offered some deals on stereo equipment that no one could refuse. I made enough money to rent a little car and fund our week vacation. We had a lot of fun that week. Did some fishing and swimming. We tented out on one of the islands most of the week. Some nights my mom or grandma would watch Latecia so we could have some alone time. We would build a big fire and then get drunk and high and make love all night.

"One day we were at the cabin and Val started copping an attitude. She was hungry and tired of eating camp food. I didn't see the problem and didn't like her nasty attitude. I told her we can drive to the nearest town 40 miles away and eat at a restaurant. That seemed to ease her mind for the moment. We got in the car and we started driving into town. As I'm driving into town, I mentioned McDonalds and she snapped at me, saying she wanted some real food. At this point, I just want her to shut the hell up 'cause she is getting on my last nerve. I tell her to roll a blunt in hopes it will help her relax. As we're smoking the blunt, I'm doing about 70 miles per hour. And this semi truck is in front of me. She's steady in my ear about how long it's taking to get to someplace to eat, so I'm trying to get to some damned food fast. I pass the semi truck by going into the oncoming traffic lane and doing about 100 miles per hour. Just my luck, just as I passed the damned semi truck a police truck passed me. I knew immediately he was gonna hit a u-turn and pull me over. I was in no mood to go to jail that day. I smashed on the gas and told Val to put the blunt out just as I seen the police lights in my rear view mirror. I knew there was no place to run so I pulled off the road and switched seats with Val because she had her driver's license. The cop pulled up just as we were done. I knew he had seen and I was going to jail. He came to Val's window and asked what the hurry was. Long story short, Val got a ticket, I didn't go to jail and we went on our way.

"The rest of our vacation was great. When it was over we went back to Val's house. I ended up keeping the rental for a few more weeks. I used it to drive to Frito Lay Company and steal a shit-load of Frito Lay products. I parked the car a few blocks away and walked to the company. Then, I found one of the loaded trucks that had the keys in it and I drove off with the truck. I loaded the rental up with chips, dips, cheeses, nuts, cookies, sun flower seeds and shit Frito lay sells. I had the trunk, back seat, floor and even the front seat full of boxes. I took the truck back to Frito lay and put it back in the spot where I found it.

"I went to the rental and dropped everything at Val's. The next day I ran into Jonah's little brother Boo Boo and we waited on a mission to come up. We didn't know exactly what we intended to rob. But we were ready for whatever. As we passed a store called Happy Hobby, I decided we would break into the store. Boo Boo really wasn't with it but said he would drive. I had him drop me off and drive to a store parking lot across the street to wait on me. The store was right below the home of the people who owned it. It was like 3 am. All the lights were off, so it seemed safe enough to me. I went to the side door and pried it open partially with a crow bar. For whatever reason, the door wouldn't pop open. I went into the store and grabbed about four boxes of these new, expensive gas-powered remote-control cars. They cost 300 dollars each and more for each one. I took them outside and went back in for more. I was looking for expensive things. I found a universal remote that is used for gas-powered planes that cost 700 dollars. I grabbed that and a few gas-powered planes. Then I took this huge monster truck and a few more gas powered remote control cars.

"I flagged Boo Boo down and he came over to pick me up. We loaded the truck and I wanted to go back for more. But Boo Boo didn't want to stick around. We left and on the way to Val's I noticed a gas station that was closed. What caught my eye was the big storage cooler that holds all the 12 packs of soda outside. I pulled right up to it and we used the crow bar to bust open the lock. We loaded about sixty 12 packs into the back seat and hauled ass. Boo Boo got a few of the remote control cars and 10 of the 12 packs. I gave Jason one of the gas powered cars; we used to race each other with them. The things were fast. They could reach speeds of 60 mph. I sold the planes and several of the other cars. Finally, I took the rental car back.

"There was a guy who moved in a few houses away from Jason. He was a young guy in his 20's named Chad. Dude used to steal cars and re-do the VIN numbers. He had a nice-ass SS he owned that he did this to and had registered in his name. Chad swore he was the best thief ever. Everyone who knew me told Chad he wasn't on my level. One day he challenges me to a night out to see who was better between us. Him and I head out together around 1 am on foot. We had a flashlight and 2 screwdrivers only. The plan was to hit as many cars as we could and to come back with the most. The very first parking lot we went through, I seen a Yukon truck with tinted windows sitting on some nice-ass rims. I started heading for it and Chad said to leave it alone.

"I wasn't hearing none of that though.

"I approached the truck and slowly walked past it to check

out the scene. As I got past it, a black dude about 6' 2" and about 270 pounds jumped out of the driver's side. I was thinking how lucky I was not fucking with the truck when the guy asked, "What the hell you doing?" I told him I wasn't doing shit. At this point Chad is nowhere to be seen. The guy says, "Why you checking my ride out?" Before I say anything he raises a gun and lets off a round, grazing my shoulder. I fell and landed on the same shoulder. Next thing I know, the dude's on top of me beating me with his pistol. He gets off of me and while pointing his gun at me, he's yelling for me to run. Hell, I couldn't even get up. My arm was fucked up and so was I. I got to my other side to get up and run. When I got up, I ran towards his truck in hopes he wouldn't shoot in the direction of his truck. I got behind a house and lied down. It wasn't until then that I realized I shit all over myself.

"I was in so much pain the only thing that made me get up and head home was the thought of the police showing up. Lucky for me, I wasn't far from Jason's. When I got to Jason's block, he and Chad were heading for me. I asked why the hell Chad left me and he said he had gone to get help from Jason. Said he wasn't trying to stick around when the bullets were flying. To a degree I seen his point, but I was still mad. I went to Chad's house, left my shitty clothes outside and went inside to take a shower. Jason brought me some clothes. I crashed on Chad's couch that night. I was in plenty of pain and knew I should have gone to the hospital, but knew that if I did the hospital would call the police. I just wrapped my wounds up and went about my business. My shoulder was fucked up for several weeks to where I couldn't hold up my arm.

"After it got better, Jason and I went back to stealing from stores again. On one of our trips we passed a nice ass GT bike lying in someone's yard. I snatched the bike and threw it in the trunk. I used the bike often just to get around the hood.

"My 18th birthday rolled around, and I started checking out all the pipe shops around, since I was old enough to get into them. It was good to get back to my passion of weed. For a while, I had gone off in phases of using different drugs. I got stuck on those over-the-counter pills called Dramamine that are used for motion sickness. Take a bunch of them and they will have you all kinds of fucked up. You walk around in slow motion like one of those crazy lizards. Shit's wild. I went through phases with plenty of other pills, too.

"One day I ran into the dude I did the crack with and he asked me to borrow some clothes 'cause he got kicked out of his house. I gave him several outfits. Few days later he tells me he has been living out the ice cream truck and his boss found out; said his boss burned all his clothes 'cause he thought he was stealing from him.

"Later that night, Val and I wanted to get drunk. I only had a few bucks, so I bought this wino beer called 211. We got us a four pack. Since we only had two each, we decided to slam them both. I slammed both of mine and one of hers. We were so drunk you'd have thought we had drunk a whole bottle of 151 rum each. We started having sex on the couch. That led to sex on the floor, then the bar chair, then the kitchen table. We stopped for a brief moment to pop a pizza in the oven. We kept making love until the pizza was done. It took a moment to take it out of the oven to put it on the counter to cool. While it was cooling off, we went right back at it. Wound up on the top of the kitchen counter having sex. Her hair ended up all in the pizza and the pizza ended up on the floor, getting eaten by the dog. We made love all night and she eventually made it into her bed. Her pussy was sore and she tried using baby oil to help, but after a while she said she needed a break. I was standing strong like never before and wanted to keep fucking; she told me just to hold her for a few minutes and we could continue after that. Maybe three minutes went by and her ass was passed out. I tried waking her but she was gone. It was about 4 am and I was wide awake. I was feeling good knowing I put down on her the way I did that night.

"Till this day, I wish I would have just gone to sleep holding her that night, but I didn't. My crazy ass decided I wanted revenge on the guy who owned the ice cream trucks and burned my clothes. I got dressed and rode the bike down to the ice cream truck company. I was gonna break into all the trucks, ruin all the ice cream and then set all the trucks on fire. Before I got there, it started to rain. I got there and left the bike outside the fence I climbed into one of those trucks to get out of the rain. About ten minutes go by and some guy comes up to the truck I'm in. That caught me by surprise. He asked me what I was doing and I lied, telling him I got kicked out of my house; said I had no place to go and just wanted to get out of the rain; told him I knew the boss. Come to find out this guy was the security guard and lived in a trailer on the property. Dude seemed straight though. As we were talking, a cop car pulled up at the gate. I told the dude there was a stolen bike out there and I probably had warrants. I had my wallet on me with my ID card and hid that in the truck. The guy tells me, don't worry, he will get rid of the cop. Every bone in my body was telling me to haul ass. A few minutes go by and the dude gets to calling me over after the cops leave. I get over by the fence and this clown grabs me in a bear hug and starts yelling. The damn cop didn't leave he just pulled away a few yards so the building would block my view.

"I was arrested and put in the car.

"The security dude gave him my wallet and told him the bike was stolen and that it was mine. I denied the bike was mine but was arrested for criminal trespassing and warrants I had out of Ozaukee County for the shit I did with Paul and Shorty. I was booked at the Milwaukee County Jail waiting transport to Ozaukee County. I used my one phone call to call Val but got her answering machine."

LOCKED UP

I actually got my nickname Angel after that. My mom had come to visit me and the CO said to her that she was there to see her Devil Child. She told him, "I'm here to see my little Angel." The name stuck and that's what I'm known as ever since.

DEBRA HILLCREST, ANGEL'S MOTHER

"I left a message telling her I was in jail. Later after I was booked I tried calling her collect but there was a collect call block on both her phone and Jason's. I ended up calling Yo's house and his sister wouldn't accept the call 'cause he wasn't home. I finally got her to accept my call with the promise I would give her some subs and amps she wanted. I had her call Val for me 3-way. Val was in disbelief and sick about the whole situation. She said she already contacted the phone company and the block would be lifted from the phone within the hour.   I let her go and told her I'd call directly.

"It took only two days before I was transported to Ozaukee County Jail. Ozaukee County Jail is mainly for holding people facing Federal time, but they also hold state offenders. I was housed on a tier which was strange 'cause the tiers were usually for federal prisoners. These guys have serious charges and are looking at life in federal prison. I was only facing 75 years max in a state prison.

"The tiers are set up with two floors. Each floor has eight single-man cells. There is a day room with several tables, a

Bowflex machine and a TV on a stand. Guys could stay out their cells from 8am to 11 pm. There were a couple of showers and a phone we could use any time we wanted to. No officers were inside the tiers, but they were in a control room behind tinted windows where they could see into all the tiers. They had a phone next to the control room we could pick up to speak to any officers if needed.

"My very first day on the tier two guys had a disagreement and went inside a cell to solve it where they couldn't be seen by CO's. Not more than three minutes later one came out and was so busted up it looked like his whole head and face were made up of dozens of golf balls. At that point I knew to stay on point. I went to court the first week and was given a 5,000 dollar bail. Unfortunately in Wisconsin, you have to pay the whole amount because they don't have bail bondsmen like some states where you only have to pay ten percent. The good thing is you get all your money back except for court fees once you're sentenced. With a 5,000 dollar bail, I just knew I'd be getting bailed out quick.

"I got on the phone and had Val call several people 3-way for me so I could get out. All the people I thought were friends gave me lame excuses as to why they couldn't help. Only family I had to ask was my grandparents. My grandma would have got me out in a heartbeat if she had the money but she didn't have it. My grandpa could have got me out if he wanted to make some huge sacrifices, but he didn't. I couldn't believe I was stuck in jail and lousy 5 stacks[17] was keeping me in there. Time passed where I told Val she was gonna trick for me to get the money I needed. My family's rich friend Don had wanted to get with Valerie when she vacationed there with me. So I told her to call him and to arrange something with him to get the money. He agreed to give her the money if she agreed to go and stay with him for a few weeks. I was all for it at first. Then Val made a comment about letting him lick her pussy and I snapped. It wasn't the act itself that made me so upset, but the fact that she said something like that without even getting the okay from me first. After I went off on her, she got mad and said she wasn't doing it.

"That ended that.

"We were on the phone so much the phone company shut off her phone when her bill got to 3,500 dollars and she couldn't pay it. Of course, her dad got her another line but it couldn't accept collect calls.

"I got moved from my tier and put inside a dorm. Basically it's just a big dayroom with about 20 bunks in it and no cells. There weren't many people in the dorm, only about 6 when I got there. At this point I had seen the investigating officer several times where he was trying to get a confession out of me on several crimes. Paul, his wife, Shorty and Mariah all blamed me for everything. Every time the investigators asked me about one of the crimes I would just say, "That's just ridiculous." They were trying to hit me with burglary while arming myself, car theft, attempted car theft, credit card fraud and a sawed off shotgun. Lucky for me, the guy, Daniel Dawson, refused to press charges for his stolen credit cards, and the sawed off shotgun charge couldn't stick cause it was found at someone else's house. I was still facing 75 years, and knew I would be spending several years in prison because of my criminal record. I had that mentality where I didn't care about shit because of the situation.

"When I got put in the dorm, I immediately made a dude move to different bunk so I could have his. His bunk was the top bunk right next to the pay phone and directly right in front of the only TV which stood on a stand on the wall. I could lay in bed while talking on the phone. I could also reach the TV from the foot of my bed to control what channel it was on. All the guys in the dorm were short-timers waiting to go home and not looking for any trouble. I got pretty tight with a young kid who had the top bunk next to mine. Dude was a clown and kept me laughing. We played cards a lot and he worked out with me every day. It was a Latino guy on my bottom bunk. We got along well and played a lot of spades together.

"I had a few words and close calls with new guys who came into the dorm. This one night the little kid and I were up real late. A big dude had just come to the dorm and the nurse brought him medication. My little buddy started clowning him saying he looked like a horse and he was taking Special K pills. Then he started making horse noises. We were in tears laughing so hard. Dude got mad and stepped to my buddy talking crazy. My buddy ain't but 16 years old and 100 pounds at the most. He didn't even belong in adult jail. This dude's like in his mid-to-late 30's, 6, 2" and at least 200 pounds. I wasn't going for that shit. I jumped off my bunk with pen in hand, got in dude's face, and told him I'd give him all the trouble he wanted if that was what he was looking for. Then I told him I was facing 75 years, wasn't going home any time soon, didn't give a fuck about no charges and I'd put that pen through his neck if he didn't take his ass back down to his bunk. Dude went back to his bunk mumbling about how kids these days are crazy.

"A few days later, I was playing Spades with the young kid against my Latino bunkie, who must have been having a bad day 'cause he started talking real stupid to me. Next thing I know, he slams his radio on the table, stands up and tells me he will fuck me up. I tell him to go off into the shower room where there weren't any cameras so we could throw down. Dude swung on me and we went blow for blow. We were going at it for a good 7-8 minutes non-stop when the police started yelling on the intercom for us to break it up. Neither of us paid any mind to them though. Finally, about ten of them came rushing into the dorm, tearing us off each other. One of the guards stomped on my toe with steel toe boots and had me hollerin' in pain. Had to get x-rays on my toe and found out the CO had chipped the bones in my foot. The Latino and I both went into confinement. It was by far the best challenge I had ever had in a heads-up fight. I didn't even understand why we'd had the fight, so I asked the dude. He said he didn't know himself. He had a busted lip and both his eyes were swollen black and blue. I didn't have any swollen eyes but had a bunch of knots on my head and a swollen lip. Neither of us had hard feelings about it. I was put on another tier when I got off confinement. I was there for maybe 10 days before I got moved to another dorm.

"During all the time that passed, Valerie was writing to me daily, sending canteen money and visiting. We still talked on the phone daily 3-ways. My grandparents were in the process of getting a title loan on their boat so they could bail me out. I met a guy who helped me file a motion for bail reduction and the judge reduced my bail to 3,500 dollars. I still couldn't get anyone to post my bail. After about another month I filed for another bail reduction and received a reduction to 3,000 dollars. A few days later I was told to pack my property. When I asked the CO where I was going he told me "home." I figured my bail was posted so I gave away all my property. They get to walking me down a hall and take me to a tier. Shit had me .38 hot 'cause I gave away my radio, clothes, hygiene, food and everything else I had. I had talked my grandpa into installing two phone lines in his house – but in my name. I talked to the phone company and they installed the lines. I had my grandpa call forward one of the lines to Valerie's house so I could call her but the charge would go on my bill. The other line I'd use to talk to family or have forwarded to someone else's house. I'd hook people up every day with calls for canteen. Within one month I ran my bill to 3,000 dollars and the phones were disconnected.

"I spent most of the time gambling on dice, Poker, Spades or Dominoes. There were Outlaws on my tier and I was real straight with one called Kid. He was an old-school biker facing all kinds of federal time. There were two guys on the tier who didn't like me for some reason. One day, I was playing chess with Kid with my headphones on with my back facing the TV. Well Kid's lips were moving, so I removed my headphones to hear what he was saying. He was saying one of the guys kept blocking the TV. He already didn't like the guy and he was waiting for him to give him a reason to kill him. I didn't want Kid getting jammed up anymore than he already was, so I told him I'll handle it. I yelled to the clown, I told him to stop blocking the view of the TV. Then I put my headphones back on and went back to my game of chess.

"A moment passed when Kid started moving his lips again, so I removed the headphones. This clown had come up behind me from the TV talking shit. Dude said he was gonna sell my ass for a pack of smokes when we go to prison. Kid started to get up but I stopped him. I told him to hold my radio down. Then I told dude I'd be up in my cell if he wanted to see me. I went up to my cell and started pacing. Dude popped up in front of my cell and I told him if he stepped one foot inside my cell he was getting fucked up. I was still pacing my cell and when I turned my back dude was just entering my cell. I ran at him and hit him as hard as I could with a shot to the face. I watched the dude fall backward damned near falling over the rail of the top tier and his face leaking blood everywhere. I was so mad I started cussing him out and his buddy, telling them I'd beat both their asses. Seeing dude standing there bleeding all over the place in front of my cell made me even madder. I picked up a pencil and told him to clean that shit up from in front of my cell.

"He went to his cell dripping blood the whole way. Then he came back asking why I did that to him. I was ready to kill the dude 'cause he was making me more mad. I told him to go tell the police on me 'cause he looked like a damned snitch. He walked straight down to the phone, picked it up, and then told it all. Police yelled "lock down" and I was just about to try to clean the blood from in front of my cell , but Kid seen it and said, "Just leave it and don't worry."

"We all locked into our cells and not two minutes later the police were at my cell asking questions. I told them right away I did it. They took me to a holding cell and him to the hospital.   After about two hours, an official comes to me and asks, "What happened?" I told him the dude threatened me and then attempted to enter my cell so I decked his ass. And I'd do it again! He kept asking me how many times I hit the kid 'cause he didn't believe one hit caused him to need 11 stitches in his cheek. My knuckles split him open good.

"I don't know what Kid said, but he told everyone on the tier to write a statement on my behalf. The official ruled it self-defense and moved me back to my tier. All the guys were cheering and calling me Little Tyson. I didn't have any more problems after that.

"I actually got my nickname Angel after that. My mom had come to visit me and the CO said to her that she was there to see her Devil Child. She told him, 'I'm here to see my little Angel.' The name stuck and that's what I'm known as ever since.

"A new guy got put on our tier and he told me how to get my phone lines hooked back up by paying them bills in full by using a false check number over the phone. I did what he told me and both my lines were activated. They only stayed on for about 2 and half weeks before the phone company realized they were bogus. I ran my bill from about 3,000 to about 5,500 in about 17 days. During that time, Valerie and I started having problems with our relationship because she was seeing a dude named Pat to hustle him for money. I was cool with that but some shit happened where he snitched on his friends and ended up living with Val. I wasn't cool with that. We broke up at that point. I finally ended up calling up Heather to see how she and our son Austin were doing. We were back talking regularly in no time.

"Only a few weeks went by and the CO told me to pack up. I was going home. I wasn't gonna be fooled again this time, so I kept my property. They walked me out the door to my mom waiting on me with a fresh set of clothes. Heather gave her the money to come bail me out. I sat in jail 9 months being hardheaded and refusing to ask the one person I knew could get me out. Of course we ended up getting back together. Hell, since we started dating when I was 13 it has always felt like we were together, even when we weren't. We had moments when we felt we needed breaks from each other.

"While I was out on bail, I was getting into all kinds of shit. The first week back, I nearly ended up in damned jail again. My dumb ass stole a bottle of liquor and got chased 6 blocks by about 8 employees of the store. I got away though. Heather and I were doing better than ever. I spent most of my time around her and our son. We both knew I'd be going to prison for a while, so we made the best of the time we had. I was still doing my thing, selling weed and running the streets. Only difference was she was usually with me. I got her to start partying, smoking weed, drinking and taking X pills. I asked her to marry me 'cause I knew we belonged together if we were able to get past all the shit that we did over the years. Of course, we both wanted to wait until I got out of prison first.

"We talked about experimenting with a threesome with another female. She told me the female would have to be fine as hell and my first thought was Valerie. I was a little worried about mentioning her though 'cause Heather knew I'd been sleeping with her and I thought she would be against it. I threw Val's name out there and she smiled about the fact that Val's name came to her mind also. I made it happen and we started a crazy love triangle. Things were great between all of us. Of course, I was really happy. I truly did love them both and tried to keep them both happy and treat them fairly. Val was still with Pat and he lived at her house, but we worked around that.

"I was still cool with Jason but felt he wasn't there for me while I was in jail. So I ended up getting tight with Val's other brother Steve and hanging out with him more. Before I went for my sentencing, I introduced Steve to all my suppliers and dudes I sold weed to. I let everyone know he would handle things while I was gone. I even gave him my cell phone so nothing would change. Of course, his ass fucked all that up within the first week I was gone. None of those dudes stood by my side when I went to prison. That shit really fucked me up because I was always there for them and doing for them. Finally, I realized they were all users of people and accepted it for what it was."

CRANKY CAPONE AND THE SIMON CITY ROYALS

I ended up hooking up with a gang called the Simon City Royals. It was a brotherhood, a family, a way for me to be embraced with the love I craved. We are labeled as a gang but to us we are not a gang; we are a brotherhood – a family. A lot of people join gangs in prison for the protection it provides.

ANGEL MILES

The Simon City Royals were originally a Chicago street gang that spread through the Midwest. They started off as a 1950's-era "greaser" gang with slick hair, flashy jackets and switchblades. Back then, they were known as Simon City, named after a local park in the Humboldt neighborhood from which they came. Word on the street, for what that is worth, has it that they have recently been involved with the corruption of penal institutions in order to smuggle drugs, most notably in Milwaukee, which was under the leadership of Donald Schultz, also known as Prince Cranky or Cranky Capone. Schultz was and is the Regional Prince of the Simon City Royals gang.

"Gang" carries an ugly implication for the members of the Royals. They prefer to see it as a family for those who need to be embraced in a cold world full of people who would just as soon hustle or "play you out" as soon as help you out. They refer to each other as "brothers" and perceive themselves as royalty in descending order, from the Prince on down. The police and media, however, do not have the same sort of perception of these associates. Newspapers report that the gang has been involved in smuggling activities that have supplied Wisconsin prison inmates with drugs, tobacco and pornography via CO's who were indoctrinated into the gang or otherwise bought off. The police believe they were involved in beatings after an "S.O.S." (Smash on Sight) order was issued for individuals not cooperating with their operations. The Royals have also been accused of having been involved in theft, burglaries and loan-sharking activities.

Schultz is in the Columbia Correctional facility in Portage, Wisconsin for his associations with the Royals and the crimes of which they are accused. He is kept in Administrative Segregation due to his security status and reputation as a gang leader. He maintains his status in the Royals, however, and his allegiance to Miles as Miles does to him. Here, he describes how he and Miles' lives intersected:

"… Now as to Michael … obviously you know about the gang stuff. Well he got into it while in prison as I was involved with it on the streets. Something I did was writing to these brothers who were incarcerated. I can't recall if I wrote him first. I think he was in Oshkosh Correctional Institution at the time. It was maybe the end of or mid- 2004. I just know my youngest was not yet one and Michael came to her first birthday. Got her some noisy toy she loved. He was real good with her. Shit he was real good with kids, period. Anyhow I'm not sure exactly when he got out, but I was at work when I got a page on my pager. See I have guys page me when they get out so we could meet. Couple of days later or it might have been that night me and Jo Jo went to Michael's mom's house which was then in South Milwaukee. We met Michael and his mom and her boyfriend. Honestly my first impression was he seemed sneaky. But later I realized his heart was all there. If he loved you he gave you his all. And he was down to do whatever so when I was told he shot a cop I didn't doubt it. Of course I was saddened that his presence wouldn't be. Like now how he wouldn't accomplish greatness. He's respectful when respected and caring as well as a goon. He had this kid-like sense of humor that made everyone love him. When he got locked up I felt bad because our last conversation in person was my bitching at him for owing money. We weren't that close either. He mainly hung with JB a.k.a John Brass who ran the group in Milwaukee. And Proof and Fro. He only came by me for parties and get-togethers or ink. But it was me who wrote him and accepted his calls ... that, when a bunch of guys were together, got them to sign cards for him. Once I asked everyone to pitch in money for him, which later got stolen. The guy I gave it to send it to him put it up in his house to go party that night. Well, the only person who saw it (JB) took it and spent it. What a friend! I even got a bunch of the guys to get tattoos for Angel. Nothing too fancy. Bars with "out of sight, never mind" in it. I've grown to love Angel as if he's my own family. Anyhow, he actually called the night of the shooting to tell me what happened and to say sorry. The cops came to question me at like 6 a.m. as to why he called in case they made it seem we were proud of what he did, that we honored him for it. When, in fact, we honored him for not being there. See, when a brother dies, we give him a title and a special ceremony, gave him his flags, of course, another brother accepted them and we gave Angel the title of 'Sir'. This was all done for a brother who was gonna be greatly be missed. I even hung up all the photos I had of him and the flags in my hallway so when people passed them they'd never forget him. See to me it wasn't a gang. It was having hundreds of brothers. We, or at least I, tried to be there. Of them all, it saddens me that a lot of those guys aren't there for Angel now. A lot of the guys on my case blame Angel for their getting locked up when what he did didn't put us in the eyes of the police. It was what JB did before they went to Florida. I won't be in here forever ... 13 years unless I get my sentence modified to 3 to 5 years. And if Angel will trust me with his Baby Momma's info I will do all I can for his son. Even if I got to send money in the mail as so the Baby Momma don't know where it's coming from. Angel means a lot to me. When I first got locked up he did more for me in there than anyone out there. I'm doing my best for him to let me in, but I feel he don't trust me or doesn't want to let me in. But I won't give up! This not hearing from him for months sucks too: Having to do the run-around to get mail to him."

Miles relates how he ended up involved with Simon City: "Time seemed to fly by fast for me. Hell, I guess that's what's to be expected when a person isn't sober from drugs or alcohol for more than a few minutes each day. My day for court arrived and with dread I headed there to face the music. When we arrived at the court house my mom and son went into the court room while Heather and I sat in the car to talk. We blazed a fat joint and talked about our future. I was nice and high and started to have a change of heart about going into the court room. I told Heather we could just leave but we both knew it would catch up to me eventually. Yeah, I could have gone on the run; maybe even gone into hiding for some years, but I wanted to get it over with so I could move forward with my life. I was ready to face the music. We went into the court room and I gave each of my family members a hug and a kiss before going in front of the judge. It was sentencing day for Paul too and he seen the judge right before I did. When the judge sentenced him to two years in prison I was pretty happy because I figured I'd get the same. I had credit for 9 months I had already spent in jail. So I knew with two years I'd be home in 15 months. When the judge gave me 3 years 4 months I was pissed. I gave my family one last look over my shoulder as the bailiff escorted me to a holding cell.

"Paul and I ended up being put on the same tier at the jail. We didn't have any beef but he knew I wasn't happy with him. It only took a couple of days before I was transferred to Dodge Correctional Prison. Dodge is just an intake prison that everyone goes to so they can be evaluated. The classification team evaluates everyone and decides which level of security threat they are. There are only three levels, which are high, medium and minimum. If you're high, you will be sent one of four maximum security prisons. If you're medium, you will go to a medium security prison and if you're minimum you will be sent to minimum security prison.

"Since I wasn't a violent offender, I was eligible to go to boot camp. That meant I'd be released early if I completed if I completed the boot camp program. This program was a minimum of 6 months long but there was about a year waiting list. I spent a few months at Dodge. Mostly I spent that time writing letters and gambling. I thought I was the rawest spades player ever 'cause I was always beating everyone in every juvenile facility I was ever in and adult jails. My first four months in prison I found out quick I had a lot to learn. Every canteen order I was paying out 50 dollars or more to guys busting me up on the spades table. Before long I was able to count the cards and remember every single card that was played. I literally paid to perfect my game. I lost a good chunk of money throughout them four months but the experience and knowledge I gained during that time has allowed me to make a lot of money over the years.

"I ended up getting moved to the annex building at Columbia Correctional in Portage. The prison was a double-max security prison. The same prison Jeffery Dahmer was killed at. But they were housing guys who were waiting to go to boot camp also. I thought it was a pretty decent prison. Had a nice outside rec. yard with basketball courts, football field, horse shoe pits and a running track. There was also an indoor gym with weights and stuff. I'd get visits almost every weekend. Mostly it was Heather and my son, but she would bring Val, my mom, and grandma on occasion. Grandpa came a lot also.

"One time I was visiting Austin and Heather when the officer said he needed to speak to me and pulled me out of the visitation room. I thought I did something wrong. Then he told me my mom just called the prison and wanted to notify me that my grandma had just passed away. I was in disbelief and was unable to hold myself together. When I went back out by Heather, she asked me what was wrong 'cause I was in tears. I told her and she tried to console me. She really loved my grandma too, so I knew she was hurting also. I ended my visit 'cause I wanted to get back to my dorm and call my mom. I cried for several hours that day. I couldn't go to the funeral, but Heather was allowed to bring a tape of the funeral for us to watch.

"All the guys waiting on boot camp got shipped to Jackson Correctional Institution for some reason. It was straight there. I ended up hooking up with a gang called the Simon City Royals. It was a brotherhood, a family, a way for me to be embraced with the love I craved. We are labeled as a gang but to us we are not a gang; we are a brotherhood – a family. A lot of people join gangs in prison for the protection it provides. That wasn't the case for me though. I tend to get along with mostly everyone and when I have beef I like to handle it myself. For years the Royals were having internal problems because of the separate beliefs people held. It's not my place to go into details on the matters though. What came from it was the Royals splitting into three separate groups who each had their own beliefs. One group had racist beliefs and followed Aryan ways. One group branched off with Latin Folks. Then there was my group who did not follow Aryan ways and ain't trying to branch up with Latin folks or anyone else. We stand on our own.

"Shortly after I got to Jackson, my cuz Paul was transferred there. I thought about how best to handle the situation, 'cause the fact was that he snitched on me – and I decided to embrace him as the family he was. Although I forgave him, I never did forget. I also let it be known to the Royals that he did snitch on me. I did this only so they would be aware. Paul was accepted among us only because I asked it to be that way. I spent most days playing basketball, working out or gambling at cards. For a few weeks, I got hooked on some pills that made me sleep days away at a time.

"Finally, I was transferred to a boot camp. That shit was

crazy. When we arrived, they left us in the van by ourselves. Then a drill sergeant comes up opening the van door, yelling for us to get out. For the next hour we heard non-stop yelling at us, directions, orders, and madness. Boot camp wasn't easy at all but it wasn't impossible to do and get through at all. The routine was easy 'cause all we did every day was work out, clean, eat study and sleep. More working out than anything else. We only got about five hours each night to sleep. I already had screwed up back from falling out of a 2nd floor window and the working out constantly wasn't helping none. I could deal with the pain 'cause I was used to that, but the pain kept me tossing and turning all night. I was lucky to get an hour of sleep every night. A guy named Chad I knew was at boot camp with me. He told me he was quitting the program for medical reasons due to having a bad knee. He said he had done the boot camp program years ago and knew if he quit due to medical reasons they would have to classify him as minimum security risk. I got to thinking about that for a few days. I wanted to get my life together so I could stay out of prison and be there for my son. At that time I knew had I completed the boot camp program and gotten released early, I would be going right back to the same exact lifestyle I left. If I quit the program and went to some work camp, I could learn some job skills and make some money. Plus I'd be able to save up money to have for my release. I told Heather on the phone that I was quitting boot camp and she was not pleased. I wasn't able to explain my reasoning to her because our phone conversations were recorded and listened to by staff.

"When I seen the people about quitting I told them it was due to back problems. They asked if that was the only reason I was quitting and for some reason I blurted out that I just didn't want to be there no more. Well, they discharged me but it wasn't a medical discharge like I intended to get. They said not wanting to be there wasn't a medical reason. I was classified medium security and transported to the St. Croix County Jail. At least I think that was the name of the jail. Chad and 2 other guys that quit boot camp were moved with me. We were sent there awaiting transport to a prison.

"It ended up being a month wait. We ran that jail while we were there. The inmates all looked up to us 'cause we did what we wanted and kept the CO's in line. First day I was there I was put on a wing with one dude that came with us and the others were put on the wing next to us. CO tried putting us in separate cells with other inmates. Him and I booted that idea of theirs and celled up together in an empty cell. The CO's didn't stay on the wing so they didn't even realize right away. After a few days they said we had to move to the cells that were assigned to us, but we refused. When they came on the wing I started throwing cans of Magic Shave at them. I forget what happened but I was put in an observation room. I didn't care. All I did was workout and sleep. Boot camp had fucked up my head 'cause there were nights I would wake up screaming thinking I was still there. At boot camp they would wake you up yelling and you were expected to yell and stand up and stand at attention at the end of your bunk. I was doing that for several weeks after at the jail. After a few days I was moved to a confinement cell and able to use the phone. I tried calling Heather but couldn't get a hold of her. I called Val and she said she wasn't fucking with Heather no more because Heather was drunk and kissing on her brother Jason at the bar. When she told me I was pissed.

"That night I wrote Heather, breaking up with her. She wrote back saying Valerie had lied but since I wanted to believe her I could be with the lying bitch. After that letter I broke up with Val too. I didn't know who was lying and really didn't care no more. They moved me to the wing with my buddy Chad and I let the CO know I wasn't gonna be bunked up with no one but him. I moved in his cell. We spent our days working out, playing cards and flirting with the girls. The girls' wing was next to ours and we could see them through the key hole on the door that separated the wings. We would write them kites and slip them under the door. Sometimes we would get them to show us their bare breasts, asses or even their pussies. We also got to go to bible/church classes and we got to see the girls there.

"I forget why, but I got moved to a different wing. I got real tight with this dude named Matthew Roge but everyone called him Philly. I embraced him as a brother and we had a lot of fun together. Spent a lot of time having rap sessions and just clownin. When they told me to pack up 'cause I was going back to prison, I hated to leave my brother Philly.

"I was taken to Jackson Correctional Institution where I stayed for only a few weeks. It was cool because I got to hang out with the people I hung out with before I went to boot camp. I was then moved to Oshkosh Correctional, which is a medium security prison. That prison is how all prisons should be like. I really liked it there. You get a key to your cell door so no one can get into your cell. The only time you have to be locked inside your cell is between 12am and 5 am on weekdays. Even then you're allowed to come out to use the bathroom. There are windows in each cell that can be opened. We could buy all kinds of stuff for vendors and have it sent into us. We could get color TV's, big headphones, electric typewriters, drawing supplies, beads, electric razors, shoes, clothes, jewelry, boom box radios, instruments like electric guitars and all types of other stuff. We could go outside pretty much any time we wanted. Didn't even have to ask either. Just sign out and put where you're going. We could go to the yard, library, work, canteen, agriculture building … more.

"The yard was huge. There are actually three yards. The yards have baseball fields, a track, horseshoe mounds, picnic tables, basketball courts and a field to play hacky sack or throw around a Frisbee. I signed up for a job in the main kitchen so I could make some money and eat good food.

"I met several Royals while I was there. I hung out with them often when I wasn't busy working or doing my own thing. I ended up switching my job from the main kitchen to the unit kitchen I was housed at. It was much better because it was less work and I could cook anything I wanted. Plus I had success to a lot of fruit, juice and sugars so I could make a lot of wine or what we call hooch or buck. I was doing good for a while until I started getting crazy with it.

"I was using laundry detergents jugs to store and to make the wine. At the final point, I had so many jugs of wine that I had to store the wine in other guys' cells. One day a Royal got off DC and moved to my unit. I went to my cell and poured a jug of wine into a pitcher and got a tumbler full to give the Royal brother. I left everything laying out cause I intended on going right back to my room. When I took the cup to him I took a gulp myself. At that point the CO was doing mail so I left the cup with my Royal brother and went to go get my mail. Minutes later, the police are coming out my cell holding the empty jug. Next thing I know, they are giving me a breathalyzer test. To my surprise, I failed that dammed test. I had only drunk one gulp. The wine kicked in minutes later though. They took me to DC and that's when shit started going downhill for me.

"I started off with 30 days DC time and wound up getting a dozen more DR's and about a year's worth of confinement time. I was put on what is called a "loaf" for about two weeks. Most disgusting shit ever. They take all the food you're supposed to get on a normal tray and they grind it up into this big loaf-like thing like break. I was put in the observation room for like a month because I was acting a fool. I went through a lot of shit in there while on confinement. Nothing compared to what I'll write later in this book that I experienced somewhere else though. Only one good thing came from being on DC there. I met a guy who was writing a chick he used to date on the streets named Desiree. He couldn't get her to do what he wanted any more so he said he was done with her. I asked for her address and he gave it to me. Her and I started corresponding and do so until I was out of prison. She helped make my time go by easier.

"I was eventually moved to Green Bay Correctional Institution because of my conduct. It's a max security prison but it wasn't all that bad. I had a Royal brother named Northwest that I hung with every day. We would shoot pool every time we went to the indoor rec. room. He was a positive influence on me and encouraged me to educate myself so I could stay out of prison. I started doing a lot of studying and planning for my release.

"Since I had no place to live upon release, the prison was supposed to put me in a work-release program 6 months before I was to be released from prison. That way I could work and save money so that I could rent my own place when I was released from prison. I contacted classification and notified them that I had no place to stay upon release from prison. And I needed to be placed into the work release program. But they never did anything. The psych doctor had me on medicine for bi-polar disorder so I was doing pretty good staying focused on my goals.

"I wanted to get out and do good so I could be there for my son. Heather and I were writing each other again so I figured we would get back together, and I'd have another chance to make things right for her and our son. A few weeks before my release, the prison said I had to provide an address to where I would be staying. I had no place else to list except for my mom's. I know I'm always welcome at her place. The day I was released I had the option of taking the bus to Milwaukee or having someone pick me up from the prison. I chose the bus because they release you a few hours earlier than if someone picks you up. Of course, the prison is unorganized and tried rushing me to the bus at the last minute. They forgot to give me two weeks' worth of my psych meds and they dropped me off at the bus station even though they dropped me off after the bus had left. I ended up calling my grandpa to come pick me up.

"A few hours later my son came running up through the doors with Heather right behind. I gave them both long hugs before going out to my grandpa's van. It felt so good to be with my family."

RELEASE

After meeting up with Cranky and a bunch of other Royals, I was offered some help by a brother called JB. He was a drug dealer and offered to front me whatever I wanted so I could get on my feet. I declined his offer at first, but after more time searching for a job unsuccessfully, I finally took him up on his offer. I got a QP of weed from him and started selling. I thought that would be a solution but it wasn't getting me nowhere. Any money I made was constantly going to my mom for bills and food. Not to mention everyone in the house was hitting me up for money to buy crack.

ANGEL MILES

John "JB" Brass, jr. was the First Knight in the Simon City Royals in Milwaukee by the time he hooked up with Miles. JB fronted Miles a quarter-pound of marijuana so Miles could "get back on his feet" financially. Eventually, the two would become close friends. Aside from Milwaukee, JB oversaw Racine and Waukesha counties. His reign started in 2003 and ended abruptly in 2006. His street name was JB, which was short for Little Thug; sometimes he was known as Sir JB due to his position in the gang. He was a powerful figure in the drug game, who according to street sources, ran drug houses and sales operations in Fond du Lac, Sheboygan, Boscobel and most notoriously on Barney Street in Waukesha, where he kept both drugs and women for his pleasures. He and Miles shared an affinity for drugs, theft, violence and gambling – anything for a thrill – anything that could be consumed to make the heart race a little faster. Alone, they had their addictions and tendencies in these ways. Together, they created the sparks and explosions of two live wires touching.

Yet, sparks fade quickly – as do temporal thrills. More and stronger drugs are needed every time an addict gets high. More money needs to be gambled to get the same thrill. More booze; more women. Overall, there needs to be more money to support all this consumption. By 2005, sources state, JB was heavy into drugs. The money that was supposed to be used to operate his businesses was being used for personal consumption. He owed money to several gang members in other gangs such as the Spanish Gangster Disciples, Maniac Latin Disciples and the original Gangster Disciples. Despair set in and by mid-to-late 2005, Brass tried to commit suicide by drug overdose on at least two separate occasions. Miles, in stride with his brother, kept pace, the two of them selling drugs, racing from city to city to pick up profits and squandering them at the local casino. When sales couldn't supply their demand, Miles and Brass robbed drug houses and did home invasions.

On top of all of this, Miles did not have the necessary medicine to treat his bi-polar medical condition, a mood disorder that mirrors his life exactly. Those who suffer from bi-polar disorder can feel on top of the world one day, their minds as sharp as razors and then crash into suicidal depression the next. There can be long periods of "normal emotion," but in between is a wild ride. Without the medication that regulates the moods, someone who is bi-polar can break with reality and become psychotic, enveloped in maniacal blood lust and sexual urges. Of course, there is the classic case of someone like Miles "self-medicating" with powder cocaine and weed to simulate that euphoria they feel during manic episodes.

The problem is that the street drugs wear off and cannot be obtained with a prescription; to obtain the street drugs necessary to simulate a manic episode in the bi-polar personality, more than script from a doctor is needed. The bi-polar individual needs "plugs," skill   , courage and usually a gun: "I was concerned about not having my bi-polar medication. I asked my grandpa to take me back to the prison so I could get my two-week supply they are supposed to provide. When I got to the prison the medical department told me they didn't have my two-week supply of meds and that I could talk to my probation officer to get them. I wasn't happy about the situation but there was nothing I could do about it. My grandpa was going to take me to see my probation officer, then take me to my mom's, but I decided I wanted to spend time with Austin and Heather instead.

"He dropped us off at Heather's house. It was a place she had recently moved into. Although she was dating a guy named Phil, she was living alone with just our son. Their relationship was rocky at that point. I knew Phil and wanted to fuck him up because I felt he had disrespected me. He knew of the relationship I had with Heather and he still put moves on her while I was in prison. He had beef with me also, for reasons unknown to me, so it was lucky for us both that we never ran into each other. I was supposed to meet my probation officer that day, but his office was all the way on the other side of town, so I called and asked to reschedule for the next day.

"My first day out went pretty good. Austin and I spent time playing Playstation together. I was amazed because he was beating me at every game. These were games I used to play with him sitting on my lap, and being so little, he didn't even understand games. We had a lot of fun, though.

"Heather asked me to stay the night and, of course, I did. After Austin went to sleep, Heather offered me some alcohol. I turned it down. She pulled out a box of blunts and some weed and rolled a blunt. To our surprise, I turned them down also. I was trying to do the right thing and stay out of trouble. Later that night, Heather and I started fooling around. Right as I'm about to enter her pussy, she tells me some lame shit about how she can't go through with it. I wasn't happy at that to say the least. I had spent several years in prison was looking forward to some good sex and making up for lost time. I went to sleep.

"The next day I took a cab to see my probation officer. Not having my meds for 2 days was already affecting me. When I sat down with my probation officer the first thing he asked me was whether I was on drugs. He asked me if I was on drugs 'cause I was talking in jumbled sentences and my body was shaking. I told him about the prison not giving me my supply of meds and asked if he could get me there. His solution was to lock me up in a psychiatric hospital for evaluation. I told him if that was my only option to get my medicine then I was fine and could do without. There was no way I was going to volunteer to be locked up when I just got out of prison. So I didn't get put in any psychiatric hospital and I didn't get the meds I needed.

"I left his office and took a bus to my mom's house. That was a journey and she lived in Milwaukee, and I had never been to her house or that neighborhood. Finally I located the house. The door was locked so I had to bang on the door for mom to come open it. When she opened the door I was surprised to see her in her pajamas 'cause it was afternoon. She gave me a hug and started to show me where my room was. As we walked through the house my stomach started to turn in disgust from what I was seeing. My mom had always been an organized clean freak. As I got older, I became the same way.

"What I was seeing was very unlike my mom and was setting alarms off in my head. There was dog shit on the floor in multiple places. Dirty dishes were piled up in the sink and lying all around, the house was dirty, disgusting and it smelled. I wanted to run from the house and get as far away from it as possible. The room that I was going to stay in was even worse.

"My mom introduced her to the boyfriend that was living with her. He was a real clown that I'd never pictured her dating. I went right to work and spent over five hours cleaning my room. After that, I cleaned up around the house a little. Not long after that, my dad comes walking in the house with some beer and hands me one. It was crazy, though, because I didn't even know my dad. I only met him one time in my life before that day. He pops up like he's been around my whole life.

"I sat around and had a few beers with everyone. Later I found out another guy lived at my house too. He was on the run for robbing some store. I called up Desiree to see if she wanted to spend some time together. She was excited and I made plans for her to stay with me for a few days. I got mom to drive to Sheboygan to pick up Desiree and her son Austin. It was out first time ever meeting in person. But it went well because we knew each other pretty well through letters. We got back to the house and I asked if she wanted to go to a bar to hang out for a few hours while my mom watched her son. I still had a little money from my release. We walked down to a bar down the street. We each got a pitcher of beer and decided to shoot some pool.

"During this period we got a little physical, kissing and touching each other. After pool, we shot darts until the bar was ready to close. By the time we got back to the house, Austin was asleep. It took no time before we were in my bed screwing our brains out. The sex was great. She had no reservations when it came to sex. She only wanted to please her man, and there was no limit to what she would do to make that happen. She stayed for a few days. I know she thought I didn't like her son 'cause I was constantly on him, but I did like him. He was spoiled as hell by his mom and had no sort of discipline in his life. I felt the need to be that father figure is if I was gonna be a part of their lives. I didn't want no whiny brat around me all the time. I treated him as if he were my own son that I was trying to toughen up and discipline. It wasn't long before him and I started to see eye to eye.

"They went home and I started spending time at Heather's with my son. I'd stay at her house and watch him while she was at work. We had so much fun together. I took him to the park so we could toss the football and hang out. That day I learned how much my son had grown up while I was in prison. He could throw the ball as good as any quarterback. I was surprised how far he could throw the ball with such perfect spiral and with such perfect placement. He was better than me and only 6 years old. He was very well disciplined, respectful to others, helpful, energetic at appropriate times and very smart. I was very pleased with how good a job Heather had done raising him. I'd like to think I played a role with that also.

"I spent as much time with him as I could, but Heather didn't want me at her house so often because of her boyfriend. Things were a mess between her and I. She refused to give me any of my stuff other than clothes and my .22 pistol. Everything we accumulated together over a 9-year period, all the furniture and the stuff my mom gave us for our own place and everything my grandma left me when she passed away. Heather kept it all. The situation had me so pissed I put serious thought into burning down her mom's house and garage where I knew everything was stored. I was fresh out of prison and had nothing but some old clothes that barely fit any more. Although I was pissed, I'd have never done anything intentionally to harm Heather, Austin or even her mom.

"I was still in my "doing good" phase, so I sold the pistol right away. It was only a matter of days of living with mom that I found out she had become a crack head, and the others living in the house were crack heads too. It blew my mind because mom never did drugs and was always speaking bad of them. Nobody in the house had a job. Rent and other bills were behind and not getting paid. There was never any food in the house. The whole situation had me disgusted.

"I contacted a Royal brother named Prince Cranky to check in with the fellas since I was out. He and a fellow named JoJo came to my house to meet me in person for the first time. It was a comforting feeling to be embraced and to finally meet Cranky in person. We had corresponded while I was in prison and I had already come to have a great deal of respect and love for him. We made plans for another time and they left.

"My situation had me so disgusted I started trying to find a job right away. I knew if I didn't get some money to get out of the shitty situation I was in, it wouldn't be long before I went back to my old ways. I searched all over for a job but couldn't find nothing. My probation officer made me come in to see him every week, and every week he was on my ass about me getting a job. I wanted to get out of my mom's house so bad I asked my probation officer if I could move, but he wouldn't let me because other felons lived where I requested to move.

"After meeting up with Cranky and a bunch of other Royals, I was offered some help by a brother called JB. He was a drug dealer and offered to front me whatever I wanted so I could get on my feet. In declined his offer at first, but after more time searching for a job unsuccessfully, I finally took him up on his offer. I got a QP of weed from him and started selling. I thought that would be a solution but it wasn't getting me nowhere. Any money I made was constantly going to my mom for bills and food. Not to mention everyone in the house was hitting me up for money to buy crack.

"I wound up making a decision and asking a Royal brother called Fro if I could move in with him and his girl Tiana. I had to lie to my probation officer and tell him it was only Tiana living at the house because Fro was a felon. He approved it and I moved in with him. It was Fro's grandma's house and we weren't paying rent. My situation was somewhat better living with them. We all got along great. My probation officer was still on my ass about getting a job. Every day I was on the search for one. There were Royals who drove me around to put in applications. Tiana and Fro's sister took me around with them job searching constantly. Finally, Tiana and I got a job through a temporary service on an assembly line. It was daily work and the boss loved us 'cause we were breaking records on daily quotas.

"The job lasted only a few weeks. Tiana called in one day 'cause she was sick due to being pregnant. The job was in another town and she was my only ride, so she let the boss know I couldn't make it either. He was fine with that. Tiana called the temporary service and left a message as well for both of us. The next day, the temporary service lady called and said I was fired because I didn't go to work. I was pissed because the boss said he was cool with it, but the temporary service said I should have called them myself. Shit was stupid 'cause I was standing right next to Tiana when she left the message for us both.

"At that point, I just stopped caring anymore about doing good and decided I was all in for whatever. I was gonna do me[18] and didn't give no fuck about no probation officer, no laws, no nothing. I was sick of trying to do the right thing and not getting anywhere. I was tired of not having shit. I was tired of constantly hearing shit from my probation officer and trying to explain how hard I was really trying to find work. But I didn't just give up on trying to do good. I also gave up on life all together.

"I started hanging with JB every day. For a while, we mainly just partied at hotels. One day I was at Cranky's house and I contacted my old friend Brad who was living with his girl Lisa in Watertown. They decided to roll through and brought a friend named Amy. Brad only had a few minutes to stay but he wanted to see me because it had been a long while. In them few minutes, I had Amy all kissing up on me and pleading with me to come to her place. I was hangin' with the fellas so I didn't go, but I exchanged numbers with her. It was only a day or two before I met up with her again. We hooked up and started "dating" right away. She had a car, so to me it was a way for me to get around and hustle.

"I started getting pounds of weed and selling them to people in Oshkosh that my cousin Toya and Shawn knew. The first time visiting my cousins, Shawn introduced me to this dude and told me he was a cousin of ours. I had some powder cocaine JB had given me to get off for him. I asked this so-called cousin of ours if he knew anyone we could sell it to. He told me I could leave it with him and he could get 150 to 175 dollars for it with no problem; said I could pick up the money later that night. It was only a ball worth of coke, I wasn't too concerned 'cause I knew where he lived, so I left it with him before I went back to Milwaukee to pick JB up, get some more weed and get a rental car for the week. After all that was done, I drove back to Oshkosh with JB to drop off more weed and get money from dude for the coke.

"JB called the dude and he started running dope-fiend games right away, talking about how he left town for a vacation out of town. I told him to tell me where he was and I would come get the money. After he made an excuse for that, I told him I'd be at his house for the money and he'd better be there. I drove to his house and nobody would come to the door. As I was leaving, I stopped the car in the middle of the street, got out with a glass bottle, and chucked it through the bay window of his house. I drove back to my cousin's house and wasn't there for more than a few minutes before the police showed up there. Dude called the police saying he seen me smash his window and followed me to Shawn and Toya's house. He was even with the police to identify me. I didn't try to avoid or hide nothing. Instead I told the police straight up that dude owed me money and was trying to get me locked up. I told them that I just got into Oshkosh minutes ago and never did what he claimed. The only reason he knew where to bring them was because he was at the house before. They left and nothing ever came from that incident.

"I was blowing money so fast I couldn't keep none in my pocket. I got a plug through a person I will not name, getting cocaine at 500 dollars to 550 per ounce. The price was so good I didn't even have to try making money. It was falling in my lap. I was already blowing 100 to 200 dollars every night on hotel rooms, 300 to 500 each week on rental vehicles, several hundred each day in bars, and several hundred each day on gas and miscellaneous shit.

"I started going to the casino to gamble and got hooked. There were days I went to Watertown to drop off some dope and get money, go to Oshkosh to do the same then hit the casino and lose thousands. It was so bad I would leave dope in several towns with people I trusted to sell it for me, just so I could go pick up more money right after losing all mine to the casino.

"I know I drove my cuz Shawn crazy. There were times I would just leave his house a few hours earlier from picking up money and I'd be calling from the casino asking how much he made for me. If he said 3 to 4 hundred, I'd tell him I'm on my way to get it, and to hustle up whatever else he could before I got there. This was a 1-and-half hour drive each way, but none of that mattered to me. I was constantly on the move from town to town. I went where the money was and JB was always down with me. We were hustling hard and partying even harder. I started to snort powder on top of all the weed and alcohol I was using. When you're getting coke at those prices, and selling it in small towns making 4 to 5 times the money back in profit, it ain't a problem to snort any quantity you want. Some nights, I'd go through an ounce just snorting it up with people I was around.

"As my habit increased, so did my need for money. A buddy of mine told me about a house I could rob for a gun and some cash. I went to the house in broad day light and kicked in the door. I found a 9mm pistol, over a grand in cash, jewelry and several credit cards that I took. I used the credit cards at multiple gas stations getting around 400 dollars out of them before disposing of them.

"I wound up in Green Bay with JB to pick up some cash that was owed to him. It happened to be the brother from prison who embraced me that owed JB. He didn't have the money so he gave us a 9MM Beretta to hold as collateral.

"A few days after that, I got a call from the same Royal in Green Bay. He wanted my help getting some cash 'cause he was in serious debt to the Asian mob. We hooked up and went on a mission to get whatever he needed to get the cash he needed. We did a home invasion on this one drug dealer he knew. It was around 3 A.M. and we knocked on the dude's door. When he opened the door, we rushed in on him. His girl was in the bedroom ass naked. She was calmer about the situation than he was. It went smooth though. We got what we wanted and left.

"When I say we robbed whatever possible, I mean just that. My buddy wasn't letting anything past us. Dude seen people in a laundry mat and had to rob them, too. It was kind of funny when he went into these people's pockets and only seen 15 cents and some gum. We left Green Bay and went to Oshkosh so I could handle some stuff. While there, we did another home invasion on a place that was a drug house. That was kind of funny, too, because we went rushing in with our guns out and the only person there was in the bed sleeping. We robbed the place and the dude never even woke up. I was surprised at finding only a half-pound of weed there. So I called my source to see why there wasn't more. Come to find out we robbed the wrong damned house. We robbed the upstairs place, but the drug house was downstairs. I wasn't about to go back to rob the right place though. Fuck that. Not after already pulling off a smooth robbery on the place above them.

"I split ways with my buddy from Green Bay. I wanted to spend some time in Watertown with my girl, Amy, hangout with my homeboy, Brad, and make some money. It didn't work out that way though. I was at Brad's for only a few hours before some bullshit went down. He had called this dude Billy who he said knew a bunch of people I could sell drugs to. When Billy got to Brad's, I wasn't trying to leave the house. I was doing coke real heavy, feeling good, and the only thing I felt like doing was spending time with Amy. So when they told me someone wanted to buy an ounce of weed, I just gave the weed to Brad and told him to handle it. They came back about ten minutes later, rushing into the house. Brad threw a fake 100 dollar bill on the table and told me these dudes gave it to him then got out of the car and ran. In my coke-induced state of mind, I flipped from chillin' to complete madness in a matter of seconds. It wasn't even about the money to me. These clowns took something from me and thought they got away with it. Nobody knew where these dudes lived, but Billy knew one of their full names. For hours I had a team of people searching to find an address for these dudes. They were calling cab companies, food delivery places, searching the internet, calling everyone in town they knew.

"Eventually I got an address and it was only a few blocks

away at an apartment. I called up a Royal Brother who lived in town and told him I wanted him to handle some shit with me. He got to Brad's within minutes. Brad wanted to roll with us but I told him no. He was trying to get his life back together and I didn't want him fucking that shit up over shit I could handle myself. I made Billy come because I needed him to show me who the dudes were. We got to the apartment complex and I took a solid three-foot steel bar that my Royal Brother had in his ride. We had to be buzzed into the main entrance of the building. The guy who told us where the dudes lived actually stayed in the apartment complex himself. So he was the one who buzzed us in. I paid the dude for his help and then went to the door of the dudes who robbed me. I was going to knock on the door but something inside me told me to turn the knob to see if it was open. It was open so I walked right in prepared for whatever. There was no one in sight but I could hear laughing and loud music coming from a back room that had the door closed. Hearing them enjoying themselves made me think they were smoking my weed and laughing about how easy it was for them to rob me. That pissed me off even more. I started to approach the back room when I heard the front door open. I saw my Royal Brother duck off into the kitchen. So I ducked into the bathroom right next to the room the dudes were in. Billy was like a deer caught in the headlights and froze up. A woman walked in and seen him standing there in her living room. She started yelling at him and asking him what he was doing there. The dudes in the room heard the noise and came out to see what was going on. I heard Billy tell the dudes they needed to give the weed back and that was all the confirmation I needed to know they were the dudes I wanted. I came out in a rage and smashed one dude in the back of the head with the pipe. The other dude was coming out the room behind me and I turned around smashing him in the face. When dude crumpled to the ground, the woman started screaming. I seen my Royal Brother run out the front door and punt the first dude in the face 'cause he was getting up. Billy ran out the apartment. An evil took over me and I smashed the woman with the pipe to shut her up. I went into a rage, running back and forth between the three of them, whacking them with the pipe. The dudes weren't moving no more but the damned woman laid there and wouldn't stop screaming for help. I went to snatch her purse and leave, but she didn't want to part with her purse. I bashed her a few more times with the purse and finally she let it go.

"I left back to Milwaukee, taking Billy with me. I later found out that both the dudes were 16 and 17-year-old kids, and the woman was their mom. They were rushed to the hospital but I never heard anything after that. I knew Billy was a liability by the way he froze up and ran from the apartment. I wasn't much concerned much for myself, but my Royal Brother didn't deserve to go down for shit I dragged him into. I took Billy to JB's place telling him he needed to lay low with me for a few days. He was trippin' 'cause he had no clothes or money, but I reassured him I would take care of him.

"I told JB of the situation and he ordered me to take care of the problem – the problem being Billy. My week was up with that other particular rental car that I had, so I turned it in and decided I would get another. I had business to take care of and didn't want to have a rental car in grandpa's name to do it. I had someone drop Billy off at my girl's house in Sheboygan. Figured that would be a perfect town to make a body disappear in since it was mostly country and woods. I knew of a lake in the middle of the woods that was said to be 100 feet deep in some spots. That was the plan. I asked Desiree if she knew someone I could borrow a vehicle from that I could use to handle some business. Everything was set for me.

"That night, all three of us stayed up all night snorting coke. It was the first time Desiree ever did coke, and the last as far as I know. It must have been about 8 A.M. when I took Desiree into her room to fuck. After we got done, I dozed off. Desiree woke me up around 9:30 am saying that Billy was gone. She was pissed because she left the door open and her son could have wandered outside. I got out of bed so fast to look for him that she knew something wasn't right. I never told her my intentions for Billy.

"I left the house searching the streets for Billy, but never found him. I called people I knew that he knew to see if they had heard from him. One of the people said he called asking for a ride, but he didn't give it to him. Word I got was that he left the state because the police were looking for him.

"I went back to Milwaukee and got another rental. I had to go see my probation officer and got caught dirty for coke and weed on a piss test. He gave me a break because I didn't deny I had used both. I wanted to lay low for a while so I spent some time chillin' at home. I always had one of my women there to keep me company. I would have Valerie stop by just so we could fuck. Mostly, though I just had Desiree or Amy staying over. I was always a "player", as they call, when it came to women. It's different to me, though. I loved and cared for each of the women I was with. I never wanted to hurt any of them. In my mind, it didn't matter what I did with other women, they should each only care what I was doing with them. If I was making them happy, then why should they care what I was doing with anyone else? I liked having different women because each of them made me happy in different ways. Desiree was my "Shorty". She was all about pleasing me and would do anything for me. She was my freak. The sex was always amazing and never denied. She was loyal to me without any reservations. Definitely the only woman I feel I should have been better to because she deserved better. Valerie was really fun to be with. She loved to have quickies in crazy places with me. Well, I still don't know what I liked about her so much. The sex wasn't all that good. I think I just liked spending time with her. Who knows? There were many things I loved about Heather.

"I didn't sleep with a large number of women throughout my lifetime. Not that I couldn't have. There were dozens of women I was moments away from fucking, but stopped myself because they were virgins. I know most men would fuck a virgin any chance they get, but I'm not one of them. I always felt that a woman's first time should be with someone who will stick around because that experience will be everlasting to them. I knew I wasn't but gonna do nothing with these women but hit the pussy and get gone. I couldn't live with the thought of them hating me because of it, so I would never fuck any virgins. There were many other females I could have slept with who weren't virgins, but I am the type of guy who will only sleep with a woman I intend on keeping around. I don't end relationships on bad terms. Any of the women I have slept with I could get out and fuck, no matter if there with someone or not.

"I finally got restless of laying low. It was boring to me and I wasn't making enough money. JB and I decided to hit Green Bay for a few days to hustle drugs. Funny thing is we ended up tricking off more money that we ended up making. It turned into us staying in hotels, hanging in bars and getting wasted. JB was slowly losing his focus on hustling and only wanting to party. I was all about partying too, but making money while doing it. He was living the same lifestyle as me, but I had more things to pay for than him. I was quick to get us out of Green Bay so we could get back to making money. We stopped in Oshkosh to visit my cousins and make some money. While there, I picked up some Ecstasy pills cause I wanted to roll with Amy. We left and went to Janesville to pick up a few more ounces of coke before going to Watertown.

"We got to Watertown and rented a motel room. Amy and her friends met us at the hotel. It was only her and I popping the Ecstasy pills and it was her first time rolling. We both downed the pills. JB and I did some lines and smoked some weed. We went to their regular bar where they knew the bartender. I'd give the bartender a gram or two of coke and she would let us sell there all night. Since Amy was rolling, I gave notice to the bartender to make sure she drank a glass of water after every alcohol drink. I didn't want her dying from dehydration.

"I was in a great mood buying everyone drinks and giving out free lines of powder. Twice, JB got into shit with dudes and

I stepped in between to put a stop to it. I bought the dudes drinks and made JB shake hands with them to squash it. I had to take JB's .38 pistol so that he didn't do anything stupid. Then Amy and her friend came out of the bathroom and some bitch started beef with her friend. I went and tried to squash that too. It was two dudes and female at the table. I spoke to them and explained I was there with my girl and trying to give her a good first time experience rolling; told them I'd keep Amy's friend in line and away from them so it wouldn't be any more bullshit. I said I wasn't looking for no problems and wasn't with no fighting. They tell me they are from Chicago and it wouldn't be no fighting, it would be gunplay. I told them it was good to see we were all on the same page because gun play is the only play I know. I bought them drinks and went back to having fun with my girl.

"I was rolling hard and feeling lovely. I thought everything was good. But when we had to leave because the bar was closing, I heard one of those bitches telling Amy's friend that she would see her outside. Now I didn't even know Amy's friend until that day, but she was there with me; therefore she would be protected by me as my friend. I wasn't trying to let shit go down, so I told Amy's other friend to go get in the van and pull it up front so we could all jump in.

"As we were leaving, this chick pushes my girl down the steps. I still remained calm and good spirited. As we are getting into the van, these chicks are standing nearby talking shit. I was the last to start climbing in when one of the chicks calls my girl a bitch and I see her taking a gun from the dude. At that moment, I lost all understanding. It takes a lot to get a person out of a good mind-frame when they are rolling. The bad part is when you get angry it is uncontrollable. I started climbing out of the van and Amy knew it was about to be some shit. I had the .38 in my hand and every intention to shoot and kill these 3 people posing a threat to us. Amy snatched me by the hood of my sweatshirt and yelled for the driver to take off. I was hanging out the side of the van and letting bullets fly.

"No shots were fired back by them.

"I assume that was only 'cause they were too busy hitting the ground for cover. We drove back to the hotel room and everyone was trippin' on me like I was the one in the wrong. I told them that next time I ought to let them all just get shot. That ended that argument.

"We left that hotel and rented another one a few miles away just to be on the safe side. I went back to be happy rolling but Amy didn't. She kept saying that I was an idiot 'cause the police station was only a block from the bar, and I also could have accidentally shot one of her friends.

"That whole week was one mess after another. I was at home and Heather said that the only way I could see my son was if she came too. I had no objections to that. I'd spend time just hanging with our son for the day. I let Heather know my girl was over there just so she wouldn't be surprised when she got there. When she arrived, it was only minutes before she wanted to get some alcohol. I took her to the liquor store and she got a bottle just for herself. I think it was E&J brandy and I got a case of beer for the rest of us to sip on. We got back to the house and Heather said she wanted an ounce of weed. So I left to go get her one. I got back with the weed and by that time Heather was pretty drunk. I'd been drinking all day by that point, drank while I was gone too, but I started killing beers to catch up with her. The music was on and Heather started dancing with me. She was grinding all on me. Amy was in the room, but I wasn't concerned. It wasn't unusual for me to dance like that with other females. All was good until Heather started kissing on my neck. I really missed her and was confused on how to react.

"Luckily, Amy didn't see this happen. As we were dancing I told Heather to chill 'cause she knew I had a girl and my girl was in the room. She tells me she doesn't care and she wants to fuck. Her crazy ass kept telling me to take her in my room and to fuck her. What's even crazier is that I was actually considering doing it. She was looking good, smelling good and it wasn't helping any that we were both pretty wasted. I forget how, but she went with Tiana into Tiana and Fro's bedroom. Minutes later Tiana comes out and tells me Heather puked all over her room. I went to check on Heather and she had puke all over herself. Tiana helped me take her clothes off and put some of my clothes on her. I asked Tiana to give a ride to take Heather and Austin home. Amy wanted to do it but I didn't want Amy knowing where Heather lived, so I told her no. We got to Heather's place and I put her in bed. I gave Austin my cell number and made sure he knew how to call me if there was any problems or if he needed me. I was gonna leave when Heather called me. Tiana said to make it quick because she told Fro she wouldn't be long.

"I went to check on Heather and the next thing I know is we're fucking. She tells me to stay the night with her. I wanted to more than ever but I also didn't want her getting her way, and Amy was still waiting at my house. Tiana started to leave. We got all the way down the back flight of stairs when Heather comes running after me butt ass naked begging me to stay. She fell down the flight of stairs. I carried her back up to her bedroom and put clothes on her before leaving again. I looked her over to make sure she had no injuries from the fall. But I was concerned leaving her. When we left, Tiana tells me Heather has got a smoking hot body and I don't know she could leave me when she wants me to stay. I didn't know how I could leave her! I just couldn't stand giving her what she wanted after the shit she put me through. We went back home and I snuck off alone to do a few lines by myself. Smoked some weed and had a few beers before Amy and I went to my room.

"While we had sex I kept thinking of two things: could she smell Heather on me and too bad she wasn't Heather. I felt kinda bad. There were many times I slept with up to as many as four women in one day but never did I think of another woman while sleeping with one of them. About 3 or 4 a.m., Heather calls me. She kept saying for me to come over and spend the night with her. I told her no and shut my phone off. A minute later Fro knocks on my door telling me it's Heather on the house phone. We went through the same shit and I took that phone off the hook. About 20 minutes later Fro knocks at my door telling me Heather is at the back door with Austin. I was pissed with her for dragging our son out at that time in the morning when he had school in a few hours.

"I let them in and had Tiana take Austin to her room and put him to bed. Heather wanted to talk. Since they came by cab I figured I'd let them stay the night. Heather wanted me to come home with her still. I said no. Then she tells me to send Amy home 'cause she is still the one sleeping in my bed with me that night. I don't know what my response was but it caused her to kick me in my junk. I smacked her in the face for it and she attacked me like a wild animal. I'm against hitting on a female, but she has always found the right buttons to push to cause me to physically fight with her. I lost my cool and gave her the ass beating I felt she needed. I took her by the throat and shoved her across the room so hard she flew and he head went through the wall. I figured that was the end of that. Not so! She was up and swinging on me before I even had time to think. For a person 5 foot and 100 pounds, she sure ain't someone a person would want to tangle with. I was so mad I slammed her on the ground and started kicking her. Fro had to pull me off her. Amy wanted to fight Heather and I told her no. Ain't [sic] anybody laying a hand on my son's mother in front of me. It was funny, though, I knew Heather would have beaten the hell out of Amy.

"I finally drug Heather outside and threw her into a snow bank. I would have left her ass out there except she was banging at the door, making all types of noise. I called her mom and told her she needed to come get her. She came right away. Heather wouldn't get in the car until I agreed to ride with them. As we were driving down the road I told her I wasn't staying with them when we got to her house. This news made her open the door and jump out while we were driving. She got up and ran off. Heather's mom took me back to my house and Heather was sitting there waiting. She would not leave.

"Finally Heather's mom told Tiana to call the cops. At that point I didn't want anything more to do with the situation, so I went to my room and went to sleep. The police got her to leave by telling her she was going to jail if she did not.

"A day or so later my mom got evicted from her house and I called some Royal brothers to help move her stuff into storage. I seen my probation officer the same day and told him about it. Then a few days later we all got kicked out of our house because Fro's grandma said she was selling the house."

THE SUNSHINE STATE

ANGEL MILES

Officer Calvin Carson of the Panama City Beach Police Department was born in Washington State and was later raised in Springfield, Ohio. He was the son of a military man, his father being in the Air Force. Carson graduated college and became a police officer who was decorated with the Medal of Honor for rescuing a toddler from drowning. His father settled in Florida and Carson switched jobs to Panama City Beach. As an officer he thrived there as well, being promoted to detective.

Carson preferred the streets and asked to be moved back onto patrol, which is what he was doing on March 27, 2005 the night of Easter Sunday when he stopped a rented Dodge Durango SUV driven by a man who had warrants out for his arrest in Wisconsin and who had been drinking whiskey, smoking marijuana and sniffing lines of cocaine – a man who had nothing left to lose.

This man had no permanent possessions, no job, no real prospects and "no place to go really." So, he and a couple of gang affiliates decided to go to the Sunshine State. By the time they had drained bottles of liquor at their hotel and continued the party on Panama City Beach's main strip, Officer Calvin Carson was on patrol, attempting to keep the bumper-to-bumper traffic moving along and trying to maintain a semblance of order among the drunken young people all around him.

It was on the corner of Front Beach and Beckrich roads in Panama City Beach, Florida that fate intervened and cornered Carson and Miles to struggle against one another and figure each one's outcome. After Fate had pointed its fickle finger, Officer Calvin Carson was found with two fatal wounds about two to two-and-a-half inches apart. Gunpowder residue was stippled on his chin and neck. The barrel of Miles' 9mm handgun could not have been more than 2 feet away from the officer's frame. The first bullet went down, from front to back, cutting through the downward aorta and some vertebrae. The second bullet tore through the lungs, liver and kidney. Carson had just enough time to make his last radio call.

Impulsive, shaking, scared, drunk, stoned and coked up, Miles tore off through the traffic and onto the beach to try to make his escape. Miles narrated the incident and his feelings in a jailhouse poem found in his cell and later introduced as evidence in court:

> *Don't take shit from anyone*
> *Cock back my fucking gun*
> *Put a bullet in the chamber*
> *Hollow point for my anger*
> *Cop pulled me over 'cause I'm*
> *I'm a stranger*
> *Little did he know he put himself*
> *In danger*
> *What the fuck was he thinkin'*

For two days str8 I've been drinkin'
Bust that lead left his ass him stinkin'
Smash the gas and hit the beach
Cops ... coming fast and filling the
streets

Gotta run and gotta hide
Keep my gun but ditch the ride
Jumped in a cab got me a lift
Found my ... brother at the bar drinking
a ... fifth

After I told him what I did
I tried to explain it's time we hid
He went to the bar and bought a drink
I seen a cop car and started to think
Oh, my God I gotta flea
All these cops, their [sic] after me
How the fuck could this be
Less than five months I've been free
Prison or Jail, I'll not see
Gotta run and Gotta hide
Stick ... to the plan, find a ride
Must leave the bar and go outside
Call my girl I need you now
Come get my ass, I don't care how
Rent a car that sounds great
Now 18 hours I must wait

Miles' story ends with his being cornered at a Spring Break motel, just as his story started with having nowhere to go and nothing viable to do from the age of eight on. So it is almost appropriate that this impulsive, damaged young man from Milwaukee, three days' drive from home, had nowhere to go, as if he knew larger forces were drawing him toward some great confrontation – his ultimate Fate. Like Oedipus at the crossroads, it did not matter which way he turned or what he chose to do; he was bound to end up with a "gat" under his thigh, his parole violated and "revocated," just waiting to kill a man – the act that would seal his fate. Everything else – in retrospect – was just a long, droning preamble: "I didn't have no place to go really. I mean there were plenty of places I could have gone but none that my probation officer would approve. I had Amy put all my clothes and some things in her car. Her sister ended up taking all my stuff and dropping it off at the Watertown police department. Till this day I don't know why she did it. Amy broke up with me on good terms; said she just couldn't deal with my lifestyle no more. I went to see my probation officer to tell him I was homeless.

"Before going in, I always checked my pockets to make sure I didn't have nothing that would get me in trouble. I found a ball of coke which I didn't even realize I had. I decided to do two quick lines and then stash the rest in the bathroom before going into his office. I came up dirty again on my piss test and he said he was putting me on house arrest. I asked where he intended to put me on house arrest since I had no place to stay. He said I'd have to do it at my mom's house. Now, I had told him the week before that my mom had been evicted. So I didn't understand how that was gonna work. He told me to go to her house and someone would check on me every few hours. If I wasn't there, it meant that I had violated probation and I was going back to prison.

"In my mind, I was pissed because he was forcing me to violate my probation before I even left his office because he knew my mom had been evicted. I didn't say nothing because I seen the set up for exactly what it was. When I left his office, I wasn't even trying to look back. I didn't even go back and get the rest of my ball of coke in the bathroom. That same day he put a warrant out for my arrest.

"I continued doing my usual. One of the Royals named MJ worked at a cell phone store, so I did all my business for cell phones through him. I was often at his store buying phones or paying for service. One night, I stopped by the store and noticed this fine-ass female sitting parked in her car. We locked eyes and I said if she was still there when I was done in the store I was gonna holler at her. Even when I got into the store I kept checking her out through the window. MJ kept asking what I kept looking at. I told him about the chick I intended hollering at and pointed her out. He started laughing and saying that was his girlfriend, Andrea. I couldn't believe my luck. Then he tells me she will be at his house later that night. I let him know I'd be over later to meet her.

"That night I rolled over to his place with my buddy Mike. It was an immediate attraction for Andrea and me. After a few hours I started to leave with Mike. Andrea spoke up saying Mike could leave but I was going nowhere. Who was I to disagree with this beautiful goddess? I pulled Mike aside, gave him my rental car keys and told him to pick me up the next day. I stayed the night there with Andrea. I was surprised to learn that she had never been in any kind of relationship of any kind, was she a virgin at 21, and she wasn't very confident in herself because she grew up overweight and only recently lost the weight. It was love at first sight for both of us. Our first night together was absolutely amazing. She was the only virgin I had no problem being with because I knew I wouldn't leave her and I wanted a future with her. We did not fuck that night but we did make love well into the next day. We went our separate ways the next day but spent another wonderful night together at MJ's house.

"JB's house got raided by the DEA, so he was on the run and sticking to me like glue. We got hotel rooms with intentions to lay low for a while. Andrea and I were pretty much inseparable from the moment we met. Only time we were apart really was when she had to go to work. Brothers would try calling me to get me to do things with them, but I wasn't wanting to leave her. If I did go out to the bar or something with them, I brought Andrea with me.

"Cash started getting low for JB and me. MJ told us we could rob his boss 'cause he knew his boss picked up all the money from 6 different cell phone shops of his and took the cash home at night. So we followed his boss home and robbed him at gun point just as he was about to get out of his car. We split the cash and all got a few stacks each. I was getting non-stop calls from my shorty, Desiree about her wanting to spend the night with me. I avoided doing so until Amy called, saying she wanted me to drive to her job in Watertown so she could get some dick during her break. I had no intentions of or desire to mess with other females 'cause Andrea was the only woman I needed or wanted. In my mind, though, I thought that Amy and Desiree deserved one last good fuck before I cut ties for good.

"I drove to Amy's job with JB and MJ. They waited in the rental car while Amy and I had our last good-bye fuck in her car. Later that night JB and I went out to a bar with my mom and got trashed till closing. I decided that I wanted to go to Sheboygan and give Desiree her goodbye fuck that night instead of renting a hotel room at 3 am. I called her to let her know I was coming and that I would have JB and my mom with me. We got to her place and I went off into a room with Desiree for the night while JB and mom crashed in the living room. Shorty and I fucked; then went to sleep. I left the next day to go back to being with Andrea.

"Up until this day, over 6 years later, that is the only thing I've ever truly lied to Andrea about. The sad part is I could have told the truth and it wouldn't have changed anything between us. Our relationship had been so pure; I guess I really wanted to believe to myself, that whole incident didn't occur during our relationship. Kinda like I had a grace period to get my affairs in order and no matter what I did during that period it wouldn't reflect on my future with Andrea. I don't wish to elaborate on the moments I shared with her because to me it would somehow diminish the memories.

"During the few weeks we had together, JB had decided we should rob this bar he knew that ran this illegal gambling lottery and would be loaded with money. I rented a new Dodge Durango and we robbed the place with a couple of others. The money got split up. A day or so later, while at a hotel, I decided I wanted to take a trip to Florida. JB was all for it when I told him. We went to them all and bought a bunch of clothes and stuff we wanted for the trip. There really wasn't any plan other than robbing some big-time drug dealer in Florida we knew about, robbing businesses and partying for a while.

"I wanted Andrea to come with us because I didn't want to be apart from her but it was her brother's b-day and she intended on being there for his party. JB and I took off for our trip. For some crazy reason, he didn't want to go with just us, so he called a dude named Deshawn Croton to have him come with us. We stopped in Chicago to pick him up. He was at his cousin's right in the hood on Martin Luther King Drive. After picking him up, JB had me stop at a liquor store to get some beer. He sent Deshawn in to get some beer. But he couldn't get it 'cause he was underage. I was double-parked but JB asked me to go get the beer instead of getting it himself. I found this odd but didn't say shit. I went into buy some beer and some clowns asked me if I had a G-pass to be in the store. I'm a skinny, young white dude with gang tats all over my body in the 'hood of Chicago, so it wasn't a surprise to me that I was being tested. I was wearing a white wife-beater and had my 9mm tucked in my waistband. I grew up hood so I wasn't concerned 'cause I knew how to conduct myself in that type of situation. I just nodded to my waist and when they seen the bulge they went about their business.

"We left and started our journey to Florida. The entire trip we drank beer, sipped on some liquor, and smoked weed. I had a ball of coke which I wasn't trying to share. I did a couple of lines each time we stopped to get gas or eat. By the time we got to Pensacola, Florida I was going on my third day straight with no sleep. We stopped at a restaurant called Crabs to eat. I wasn't eating nothing so I walked the beach while they ate. It was Easter weekend so I called Austin to wish him a happy Easter, but got the answering machine, so I only left a message.

"It was Spring Break and the waiter at the restaurant told us Panama City Beach was the best place to go for partying. So when we left we headed straight there. We found a hotel to rent a room, and then went to the liquor store to pick up a few cases of beer and a couple of bottles of liquor. JB and I hit the hot tub, taking a bottle of liquor each with us. We stayed in there long enough to finish off the bottle then went back up to our room. JB and Deshawnstarted talking to a group of guys partying at another room and decided to party with them.

"I had Andrea heavy on my mind and wasn't in the mood to hang out, so I took some beer and liquor to the truck to drink on while listening to some music and talking to Andrea on the phone. I did a few lines, finishing off the coke I had left. Maybe an hour went by and I was alone in the truck drinking, listening to music and talking to Andrea on the phone when everyone started jumping in my truck. JB said they wanted they all wanted to hit the strip and check out this bar that was supposed to be jumping. I was pretty tore up and really didn't want to go nowhere, but I also didn't want anyone else driving a rental that was in my grandpa's name. They directed me to a bar that was only about a mile away.

"When we went into the bar, it was dead with us being the only people there. Plenty of people were out on the strip and partying for Spring Break though. I drank a few mixed drinks before I finally had enough of being there. I bought 2 mixed drinks (Crown Royal and Coke) and left everyone inside while I hung out in the truck. My mind wasn't on hanging out and partying. I didn't want to be near anyone. There were thousands of people around me on the streets having a blast for spring break. I should have been doing the same, but none of it felt real to me. It was like I was outside my body and watching from a distance. I went back inside the bar to get more drinks to take to the truck. I talked to Andrea until I finished my drinks and decided I'd drive down the strip to see what was going on. As I was about to pull off, Deshawn jumped in the truck and asked where I was going. He said he wanted to roll with me.

"Traffic was bumper to bumper, moving no more than 5 miles per hour. Everyone around was hanging out car windows talking to females, getting their digits and hollering to see some tits. Deshawn was no exception. It couldn't have been more than 5 minutes after leaving the bar before I was pulled over by a cop.

"Till this day I ain't clear as to why I was pulled over, but I always suspected it had to do with racial profiling. I don't recall seeing more than three black people my whole time in that area of Panama City Beach other than the one I was with. Anyway, I told Deshawn I was gonna pop at the cop and speed off. I didn't have a license and was wasted, had warrants out for me, and had a loaded gun on me. I had no intention on sticking around. Deshawn talks me into letting things play out and say I'm only gonna get a ticket. The cop came to my window and I gave him my ID. He went back to his cruiser to run my name. During this time I gave Deshawn my phone and had him call my woman for me. I don't recall what I said. But I do remember telling her to come get me 'cause I was about to shoot at a cop and ditch the truck. Soon as I got off the phone, Deshawn got out the truck and disappeared in the crowd.

"A minute went by before the cop reached for my door handle with gun in hand and I panicked. My gun was already under my thigh where I always put it when I'm driving in case someone tries running up on me. I grabbed my gun and started shooting out the window at the cop as I sped off. I drove onto the beach a block away with police cars chasing. It was like the whole world was going off with sirens. On the beach, I put the truck in all-wheel drive and sped down the sand doing 80 miles an hour. All the cops chasing me got stuck in the sand. I seen a hotel building and stopped the truck to get out. I was so fucked up my dumb ass is on the run and have all the truck windows down and I take the time to hit the alarm on before running away.

"I got back to the strip and hopped into the back of a truck on the road. There were two guys in the cab. The windows were tinted, so I didn't know how many people were inside the vehicle. I took all the money I had out of my pockets and handed it one of the guys in the truck, telling the guys I just wanted a ride to the bar where my friends were at.

"Police were everywhere.

"Even in the damned sky.

"They dropped me off at the bar and left. I walked into the bar and tried telling JB what had happened. He was so drunk he got on the karaoke stage and started singing. I got me a drink and slammed it before getting on stage with JB. I don't recall singing though. I got him off the stage and told him what happened again. Next thing I know, Deshawn is walking into the bar. When he seen me it seemed like he was seeing a ghost. He had caught a ride from someone and had them waiting to give him a ride to the hotel. We all went to the waiting Jeep and I had to drag JB away from bitches showing their titties. They dropped us off at the hotel.

"I called Andrea and she was already on her way to Florida to get us. I ain't too clear what all happened after that. We ended up going outside to hide out and they told me they were going back inside for blankets. Next thing I know, I'm waking up in a garbage can and the sun is coming up. My cell phone battery was dead so I was gonna find a pay phone to use. As I was looking around the corner of the building a cop snuck up behind me and put a gun to my head. I was on the ground surrounded by cops and guns within seconds. They searched me, finding a pocket full of bullets but no gun. My gun was in my waist band tucked under my t-shirt.

"As they were taking me to the squad car, I kept thinking how I'd make them pay for beating on me. Before I got to the car another cop was told to escort me, and he grabbed me by my belt loop for some reason and felt the gun in my waist band by doing so. He yelled, "Gun!" and slammed me to the ground for another stomping while they disarmed me. When I reached the squad car they stripped me of my clothes, ass naked, in front of a whole crowd and then put my boxers on me.

"I was taken to the police station where I was denied clothes or food because I refused to speak to the investigators. I was put into a holding cell where they already had Deshawn and JB. Not long after that, they took them out to a transport van. A guy in a nice suit came into my cell and told me that if the State didn't kill me, he would make sure personally that I was killed one way or another for what I did. They took me out to the transport van where the media cameras were snapping photos and asking questions.

"As I was put into the van a cop was strapping the seat belt on me while another was pushing my head backwards so hard I thought he was gonna break my damned neck. We drove to the Panama City Beach court house and I was taken to the court room. I was paraded in front of everyone wearing nothing but my boxers which were hanging half off my ass. I guess here in Florida a person can be paraded into a court room basically naked and exposed. Of course, that's not legal, but the ones enforcing the law are always above the law. I was taken to Bay county jail and placed in confinement.

"Every day CO's were trash talking me, threatening me, and even spitting in the food they served me. I didn't eat for days 'cause I was afraid to. Time went by in a blur for me. Investigators wanted me to confess and threatened to lock Andrea up if I didn't. Deshawn had told them I informed her of what I was gonna do, told her about it afterwards, and she had drove to Florida to pick me up so I could get away. This was enough for them to charge her for attempt of helping a felon avoid arrest for a capital crime. It was a bad situation which I wasn't gonna let her go down for. She had only known me for 17 days! I admitted to my crime so they would leave her alone. At the time I really didn't care what happened to me. Although I willingly admitted to what I did, I never admitted to it being premeditated, because it wasn't. I never planned or intended to kill anyone. Ain't no way a person could be as fucked up as I was at the time and be able to plan a murder in a few brief minutes. None of that stopped the State from seeking the death penalty on me.

"They were so blood thirsty for revenge that they held both Deshawn and L.T. in jail on $100,000 bonds as material witnesses until they testified against me. Deshawn Croton not only snitched on me and almost got my girl jammed up too, but he also made multiple different statements and lied on me. The State scared him into finally making the right statement they needed to justify them seeking the death penalty for premeditated murder.

"During questioning, I took the solo blame for crimes L.T. committed on his own, as well as ones we did together, because I wanted to save him from more trouble. Come to find out, John "L.T." Brass Jr. had already snitched on me, and then he was released and worked with the government to set up over a dozen Royal brothers to be indicted on a number of charges. I was finally placed in G.P. (general population) after filing a number of grievances with the jail for being in confinement without justifiable cause.

"Things were going fine. My family, Royal brothers, friends and Andrea were all standing by me giving me love and support. Then out of the blue, I got taken back to confinement with false accusations that I offered some inmate $100,000 to help me escape. It was straight bullshit! Funny thing about it was the thought of escape never even crossed my mind until that happened. But once it did, I thought of nothing else. I eventually got out of confinement and put back in G.P. again. The jail guards were so corrupt that they were bringing in anything inmates wanted if they had money to pay for it. Guys were getting drugs, cell phones, cigarettes, and even pussy from female guards.

"My girl drove down from Wisconsin to visit me, bringing my mom along. She loved me so much, she didn't even hesitate to empty her bank account and sell off a lot of her belongings to make sure I was straight on canteen and she could bring my mom to see me. Visitation was behind glass windows and non-contact, but we enjoyed them nonetheless. We made plans to be married at the jail, but the jail screwed up and got the date wrong, so that never happened. I got my hands on a cell phone, 2 ounces of weed, cash money, 17 saw blades, and several packages of cigarettes. On their drive home, I called Andrea on my cell phone right after getting done blazing some fat joints. I asked her to stop at a store to buy me a phone card so I could put minutes on the cell phone. I called her about 30 minutes later to get the info for the card she bought. When I tried programming the minutes into my phone I was so high I kept putting in the wrong password. Finally after putting the incorrect code in so many times the safety feature activated and killed the SIM card. Only way to ever be able to use the phone again would be to contact the company and have them send me a new SIM card.

"I had been sawing out the metal block between the window in my cell for days. There was no way for me to hide this fact from the guys in my dorm. To keep everyone from snitching on me I made sure to try keeping everyone happy. All day long I gave away cigarettes and smoked weed with everyone for free. I had over a dozen brown grocery bags full of canteen food, which I gave away freely to anyone who wanted any. There was a dude who stepped to me about my cell phone saying he knew I had got one and he wanted to use it. I told him it didn't work. He accused me of lying so I gave it to him and said he could have it. Then the dorm runner who cleans the halls was constantly hitting me up for weed so he could sell to dudes in other dorms. I always gave him shit when he asked. Then, two days later he steps to me for more weed and I tell him I only had a couple joints left. I gave him all but one. He comes back later asking for more and I tell him I have none. He accuses me of lying, saying there ain't no way I went through two ounces in only two days, but I had! What did he expect when I'm supplying him to sell shit to two other dorms as well as supplying everyone in my dorm? I had finally got done cutting through the medal of my window so I could escape.

"I called Andrea using the pay phone and told her I needed her to drive back down to Florida right away. She had only left a few days earlier, but didn't even question my request, and came back down. I went out to visit her and mom. I told her to wait outside in her car by the bridge after she left. As I headed back to my dorm, I passed another dorm on my floor and guys were yelling to me saying, "They snitched on you." I got to my dorm, and before I could get through my cell door I seen about a dozen guards rushing onto the dorm. I noticed saw blades sitting on my bed, a place I did not leave them, and I tried to get rid of them quick. I only had time to throw them into the toilet, and hit the button to flush them, but they did not flush.

"The guards rushed my cell directly and took me to confinement. I yelled to a buddy to call my girl and let her know what happened. I was charged with attempted escape and introduction of contraband. They moved me to the annex jail and put me ass naked inside an observation unit for guys who are suicidal. They placed a guard to sit in front of my cell watching me 24-7. I was kept there for a few weeks then moved to another cell. All my property had been stolen, or so they told me.

"The cell they put me in was located directly on the side of the control room where the guards could see into at all times. The cell is actually designed to house only people with T.B. temporarily. It's more of an observation cell. There was a camera watching inside the cell so the guards in the control room could watch the feed on a monitor. There were three 3-1/2 foot long fluorescent lights inside the cell that stayed on 24-7 and could not be even dimmed. Housing me in this cell was against the law, but that didn't stop them from doing it.

"My whole world came crumbling down around me starting the moment I was put into that cell. These people had no regard or concern about my prisoner rights, constitutional rights, rules and regulations of the facility, state laws, federal laws, or anything else when it came to dealing with me. For over six months, I sat in that Hell hole being psychologically tormented, mistreated, and getting physically abused. There was an investigator named Randy Squires who was always at the jail, and he had a serious hard on for me. Between him, the warden, and the chief of security, I couldn't ever catch a break. There were times they would take all of my property for weeks at a time. They wouldn't allow me nothing. I couldn't have soap, toilet paper, writing supplies, nothing. Shit, they even would take my mattress for several days at a time, leaving me to sleep on a metal slab with no blankets. I wasn't able to send out mail or receive it. Randy Squire was just throwing my shit away.

"I wasn't allowed rec. for months. Then, when I did get rec. it was worse than being in the cell. They would keep me fully restrained. Bastards even had me taking showers while having to be fully restrained. How's a person supposed to wash up when they're shackled, hand cuffed, and have a waist chain around them with a black box on the cuffs? They often made me go weeks without even allowing me a shower. The times I was with my property I'd write grievances on issues and Randy Squire would always respond to them with smart ass comments. I would tell Andrea about my situation and she would call the jail weekly voicing complaints and concerns about my living condition and treatment. She would contact whoever possible constantly trying to get me help. The jail hated that I had that type of support coming from the streets and making trouble for them.

"One time they put a damn pad lock on my cell door and only the head honchos had a key for it. I had my people file a complaint with the board of environmental health and safety. The jail was told to remove it immediately. Had an emergency happened, I'd have been dead. There was an incident where six guards rushed my cell because I was going off about mistreatment. They first sprayed me with pepper spray and told me to come to the cell door so they could handcuff me. By this point, I'd already been sprayed so many other times it no longer even affected me. They had been mistreating me for so long I had reached my breaking point. I wasn't cuffing up for them and I had every intention of killing whoever I could get my hands on. They rushed my cell with the first guy holding a shock shield. I kicked the shield and swung at the guard trying to hit him in the throat with a homemade shank. He deflected the blow with the shock shield and the shank ended up only grazing him in the head. I tussled with them for a few seconds before they got me on the ground and shocked me with the shield.

"That incident caused me to get outside charges for

aggravated battery on a L.E.O.[19] and introduction of contraband for the shank. Another time, I went off and ended up being shot by a pepper ball gun multiple times, pepper sprayed, and involuntarily shot up with drugs inside a needle to put me to sleep. These people were treating me so bad they kept me housed in a cell for almost two months with a toilet that couldn't flush. That wasn't even the worse part. The shitty toilet water leaked into the cell on the floor constantly. It possibly would have never got fixed if it hadn't been for me voicing my complaints to my judge at a court appearance. He ordered the jail to fix my toilet and they did.

"About five months had passed since I had tried to escape. Randy Squire started fucking with me hard for no reason. They stopped letting me use the phone. I wasn't receiving any mail even though I knew for certain Andrea was sending me mail at least three days out of the week. This went on for weeks. Then they come to me and told me they approved Andrea and I to get married. They gave me the phone to call her so we could make the arrangements. I knew right away that they were up to no good. I used the phone to call Andrea and tell her the news. She was excited and wanted to come down to get married since the jail had already screwed us once before. I told her she wasn't coming down though because it was a set up. They had already put several officers on leave under investigation 'cause they knew someone had to bring the saw blades and stuff into the jail. Nothing came from that investigation though. They needed a scapegoat, and who better to pin shit on then the one person supporting me in every way?

"After I talked to her I started getting mail again, but none from her. None of my mail I sent out to her was reaching her either. I found this out because she wrote to me using a pseudonym, a different address, different hand writing, and wrote as if she was someone else. Randy Squire gave me the letter only because he didn't know it was really from her. I knew right away after reading it. We started writing each other like that.

"A few weeks later I'm up early listening to the news on my radio when I hear them say, "Accused cop killer Michael Miles' girlfriend, Andrea has been arrested in Wisconsin for charges of helping him try to escape." I was stunned and broke down in tears. These people were determined to destroy me, everything or person I loved, and everyone who loved and supported me. Andrea was transported from Wisconsin jail and brought to Florida and put at the same jail I was at. It hurt me so much to see her going through that shit just because she refused to stop loving and supporting me. I put together a care package of some food, hygiene, clothes, books, and writing supplies for her. A Sgt. took it to her dorm for me. It was never given to her though because Randy Squire seen her name on the bag and took it.

"Andrea was facing ten years max. Her public defender was a dick with no intentions to do his job defending her. The State offered her a so-called deal which consisted of five years in prison, five years of probation, to testify on me, and she couldn't have any contact with me during these ten years. It was a joke! Worse part was her public defender told her to take the deal and she gets what she deserves for being with a cop killer. The "deal" was even more and worse than they could even give her. She had never been in any type of trouble and wasn't familiar with the unethical ways the system tries to screw someone.

"Her family gave her horrible advice, telling her to take an open plea in court just so she could get the whole situation behind her and go home. There was no proof she did anything. The State claimed to have two inmates saying Andrea gave me the saw blades. It was a real joke! Visitation is conducted behind glass with no contact possible. Visitors coming into the building for visitation go through metal detectors. The two inmates were the guy I gave the cell phone to cause it didn't work, and the runner who I told I didn't have any more weed to give him. Andrea didn't like being locked up and only cared about getting out. She didn't want to wait the years it could have taken for trial, so she took and open plea thinking she would go home.

Judge sentenced her to do three years in prison. I was so angry at her family for giving her such bad advice, and just as angry at her for taking it. They weren't letting us write each other and I finally snapped after she got sentenced. I told them straight up that they either let us correspond with each other, or they would deal with me 24-7. They already seen that I didn't have any problem acting a damn fool. I done threw food trays at them, tore the camera off its perch, tore the light fixture off the wall in my cell, flooded the cell, swung brooms at them, lit my cell on fire, they didn't want to deal with me like that 24-7. The Warden agreed we could correspond and a Lt. would transport the letters between us several times each day. I had to give my word that I wouldn't give them any problems in turn to receive this.

"Things went fine until the night she was going to be taken to prison. I could see out my cell window the people going by when they were being transported to prison. Someone gave me a head's up that Andrea was leaving that night. I seen the girls all out there and Andrea wasn't amongst them. I knew the jail was trying to pull some bullshit once again. I wasn't about to let my woman leave without getting to see her one last time. I started kicking on my cell door until the Sgt. came. I asked where Andrea was and told him I already knew she was leaving that night. He told me they were gonna take her out another route because someone told them I'd go off if I seen her leaving. I let him know that I wanted her brought to the window so I could see her and say goodbye; otherwise they would see a side of me they wouldn't like. Of course, they brought her to the window and I got a few moments to say goodbye. It was heartbreaking to see her suffering. Andrea dealt with it all like a champ though. My baby didn't fold under pressure, didn't snitch, and didn't stop loving or supporting me.

"Not long after she left, I took an open plea in court on charges for aggravated battery on an L.E.O., intro of contraband, and attempted escape. I only did this because I was tired of the treatment at the jail and the judge promised to send me to prison until my capital murder trial started. I was maxed out on all my charges and sentenced to like 65 years. I didn't care! I even thanked the judge. I got moved to prison right away.

"Florida prisons are nothing like what Wisconsin's prisons are. I thought slavery was ended in the mid 1800s, but Florida has turned their prisons into the new-day slavery plantations. All that can be told at another time. I wound up in a psych. treatment unit on many different medications for bi-polar disorder. During this time I was transported back to the jail for my capital murder trial. Them months were a complete blur because I was being over-medicated and barely even knew what I was doing. I was finally sentenced to death, 11-1 and moved to death row.

"The first week I was in prison, I was upset cause I hadn't heard from my Royal brothers. The second week I get a bunch of articles sent to me by Desiree. They were news articles saying a bunch of Royals were indicted on multiple charges. All my homeboys got locked up. John "L.T." Brass Jr. had worn a wire for the Feds and set everyone up. Dudes were being indicted left and right for three years straight. All my people were locked up! For about a year, I tried corresponding with well over 100 Royals. I had plenty of money at the time so I was helping them however I could by having money put on their account for canteen or getting them magazine subscriptions.

"All that came to an end when I started finding out more and more dudes were snitching. Only person I have stood by nonstop is Prince Cranky Capone A.K.A. Donald Schultz. He is the only Royal who has always stood by me, so he will always receive that in return. There are a few others who pop in and out over the years. Only Royal on the streets right now who has done anything for me recently is my brother Hooligan. I don't even correspond with any Royals anymore unless they are trying to change their lives for the better. Gang bangin' and thuggin' just ain't what I'm about or trying to be a part of no more. I'm trying to learn and educate myself so I can be a positive influence onto my loved ones. Andrea has been out of prison and back in Wisconsin for several years now. Never once has her support or love waivered. I'm to the point now where I'm fighting my death penalty in appeals court. Some days I'd like to get off Death Row, and others I think about letting the State execute me. I never put much value on life and I guess I still don't. I always think there must be something more after death, and I'm ready for that journey if there is."

THE ANGEL'S CONFESSION

Brass: Hello?

Amtel: This is a collect call from (inaudible) from a corrections facility, using Amtel, this call may be recorded. To accept the call dial zero, thank you for using Amtel.

Miles: What's up?

Miles: They're saying I'm mildly retarded and that I might be crazy.

Brass: Yeah?

Miles: Yeah, they're talking about sending me to the nut house.

Brass: That's a positive.

Miles: Yeah, I know it brother, I'm working on it.

Brass: The problem is they will evaluate you.

Miles: Yeah, they got another psychiatrist coming to see me again, you know, it's all good though, so if you start getting some letters and stuff that sound kind of weird, don't mind them, I was talking about how I was from the [future] and shit in one of my letters.

Brass: Yeah.

Miles: I told my lawyer, I told my lawyer straight up, I said my boy, Brass ain't locked up, he out on bail right now. I said, well, he said, if you go to the nuthouse, you ain't gonna to have to worry about it anyway, or if they find you mildly retarded, then you ain't gonna have to worry about it anyway, because they can't, they can't try me if they find me mildly retarded or crazy.

Amtel: One minute remaining.

Brass: Yeah, but the problem is, you'll go to the nuthouse for the rest of your life man.

Miles: Nah brother ... you ain't understanding. You go to the nut house for five years, brother, if they don't find you competent within five years, after five years they find you, they legally find you not guilty by reason of insanity and then you stay in the nut house and if you ever get better after that five years, they let you go home, boy.
Brass: For real?
Miles: Yeah. I ain't no rookie when it comes to this shit brother.
Amtel: Twenty seconds remaining.
Miles: I'm playing all my little cards brother, don't even trip, I'm trying to make sure that happens, man. I hope you, you know, you need to do something, too, brother start talking to walls.
Brass: Huh?
Miles: Start talking to the walls and shit, brother.

Residents of Death Row spend most of their time in the cells that they call their houses, waiting for letters from the outside world, waiting for their canteen orders to arrive to supplement the two meals a day they get shoved through their bars on trays, and waiting to hear news about their cases. *(Did they get a stay of execution? Did their motion for pro se go through? Were claims for inadequate representation honored?)* If they get put on Death Watch, they know the Governor has signed a warrant with their name on it, and they get moved to a different cell for constant observation. Mostly, though, they just wait – for food, for money, for yard time, for shower time and for news from the outside. In between are unrelenting moments of tedium that they try to break up by playing chess with guys in neighboring cells and "kicking the bobo," which means joking around.

Otherwise, there is Florida heat most of the year and cold the rest. There may be running water – or there may not be. There is always tension between the guards and the inmates; there is always the fear of death. One resident of Death Row describes the physical conditions:

"Have I ever explained to you how this building is? There are six wings and two stories. A run has 14 cells. A floor has 28 cells.

Front of the cell is bars. Then there if the hallway 5' wide, then another wall. The there is a 3' wide hallway (called Catwalk), and then the outside wall that concrete. That wall has windows in it but the way they are made they don't let much air in when the exhaust fans don't work. There is no A/C. The only A/C is in the guard's station and visiting room. In the back of each cell there is 20" by 20" exhaust vent. Back side of this run is the same. There is a 3' wide pipe ally between the cells. And is where the exhaust fans are at. There are 7 big exhaust fans on the top of each wing. The problem is that only two of them are working. Those two pull most of the air through the five that not working and nothing through the cells. Therefore it gets hotter than fish grease in those cells during the day. I'm told this wing is hotter because the others don't have as many fans not working. Plus this wing points NE so it has sun on it most of the day."

The same inmate describes the impending death of an inmate:

"Oh, we hear about it when an inmate is coming up for execution. The day that the Governor signs a death warrant we hear about it. Or within a couple of days. Since they went through with Grossman's execution we are figuring that the governor will be signing another warrant soon. I did not know Grossman. I seen him around but never talked to him. When someone does get executed it does weigh heavy on everyone's mind. Because it means a friend in some case is gone and it means that someone else will be next. And no one will know who it will be until a warrant is signed. It's like someone that has cancer. They know they will die any day but don't know when. Since I've been on death row there have been five inmates executed that I had got to know. It's like losing a family member because guys in here become family. It is hard. What scares the hell out of me, Florida had executed at less four innocent men that is known so far since 1986. I may be innocent but still set here with the thought that I could be executed."

Yet another describes the constant war between the authorities and the inmates and the subtle games that are played:

"Call me paranoid if you want to, but I've been dealing with these people now for a long time and have to come to gain some insight into the DOC psychology. And I often think, "And we are the ones they have locked up?" The majority of these people here are some sadistic assholes. One young guard complained he didn't like working Death Row because he hasn't been given a chance to mace anyone yet. I'm not kidding. Went to the hospital once and a group of about 8 of them joked and bragged about beating prisoners (this is an elderly and mental patient institution)."

This is where, in the final chapter of his book – and his life – Miles finds himself, a place with no pity, no shame and no irony. It is the end of the line. For a young man who had nothing but unrestrained freedom and indulgence, it is no less than Hell. He ends up demoralized with no strength left to fight for his life.

So the Angel confesses the truth about his son; and horrible truth about Heather. Moreover, Andrea, who attempted to help him escape, has been barred from communications with him. His family does not have the means to visit him. The Angel feels he has no more fight left in him, except for spasms of madness:

"What's good? Just got back from court. That was a complete disaster. I got screwed all around the board. I wasn't at the jail two hours before I put my fist through my cell's light fixture breaking that and busting my hand all up. Told them to run it 'cause I wasn't gonna put up with their fucking shitty games. Fuckers put me in a cell and had the water shut off as well as the toilet. Fuck that! They tried me all around the board. Refused to give me my legal work and writing supplies I brought. Illegal! Had me in a cell with no working toilet or running water. Illegal!

Cell had 3 three-foot lights with no dim or off switch that stayed on 24/7. Illegal! Got a camera in the cell. Illegal! And they thought I was going for that shit! Run it! Suit up and bring the squad 'cause I'm fuckin" someone up. They tried using scare tactics telling me I was only gonna end up hurt and strapped to a table for hours. Bring it! I don't see none of that fucking shit! I let them know that scare tactic shit they can save for a cracker that ain't been there and done that. Been there! Done that! I was .38 hot brah. I told them they might as well call home to their wives and let them know they wouldn't be home for a week cause I was gonna set it off every hour on the hour just so they couldn't go home. That got their attention 'cause they know how I can get real stupid. Lucky for them there was two there who knew me and informed them that I don't see none of that shit and will dish out more than they care to see. The Lieutenant spoke to me and asked what they could do to keep me from giving them hell while I was there. I negotiated to get my water and toilet cut on, get some reading books, and to get to use the staff phone at least three times for no less than 20 minutes to call whoever I wanted for free. They agreed and I leaned my ass back. Got to call my wife for free. I loved that. Only had one problem after that incident and that was cause they brought a dude on the wing to shower. It so happened to be the same fuckin' nigga, Carlos Worlds, who snitched on me in 'O5 and got my wife 3 years in prison. I seen dude and tried knockin' my cell door off the hinges to get at his ass. No luck! What's the odds, hey? Then I get to court and that went horrible. Jail says I can get a visit from family and wife but my investigator tells them jail said no visit. Liars! I tell family I can see them at prison Saturday and Sunday and investigator tells them they can't cause prison refused the. Sorry bitch! She just wasn't trying to pay to keep them here for the extra days. They screwed me out of seeing my family! My own fuckin' defense team! Shit has me so mad I ain't speaking to them for nothing. Then I get back here to D.O.C. today and they ain't giving me my property. I don't have my fan so I'm boiling alive right now. They also put me on a different wing so I'm not by Rip no more. That's killing me 'cause that brother was helping my broke ass every week so I was str8. Now I don't have him to lean on and will be screwed. To make matters worse I left a whole bunch of my property with Rip and two other people on his wing before I went to court so nothing would be stolen or come up missing. Now I have no way to get all my shit. I'm not very happy about none of this shit. I did get to talk to my wife several times on the phone, and to me, that was worth the world. I saw her in the courtroom also. My mom, brother, and dad I saw too because those three came to testify. Broke my heart to see my lil' bro up there crying and I didn't even get to visit him. He came all the way down from P.A. When I get the $ I'm gonna send it to him so he can come down and visit me. I'm ready to end these appeals and just get this shit over. I want to see my lil' bro at least once before I die. Well, I'm burning up and need to get my sticky ass in this sink to cool off."

After cooling off for a few days, Miles became more introspective and decided to end the story of his life with this confession:

"After further thought and some new developments in my life, I've decided to make an addition to this book and give not only you readers the truth but the world the truth as well. I do not mean to imply that what you have already read is not the truth as I remember it, because it is. There are certain things I left out or tried to sugar coat for many different reasons. Some are due to me having an open case pending on appeals for my death sentence others are simply because I didn't want innocent people to get hurt by what is told. And some is because there are certain things that just hurt too much to even write about. Now that I have your attention, which no doubt I do, I suppose this would be a good time as any to get this over with. I mentioned my early years when I was only 16 and my girlfriend, at that time, Heather, was pregnant. What I failed to mention was the child she was carrying wasn't mine. Heather cheated on me and later led me to believe that she had been raped by a man. To her credit she did tell me there was a possibility that the child wasn't mine and could be the child of the man who raped her. This was told to me before he was born. At that point I did what I felt any real man should do in a situation like that; I told her no matter what the outcome that child was mine because she was not to blame for being a victim of rape. I wasn't going to turn my back on the woman I loved when she was in such a vulnerable state at no cause of her own. It was understood that I was the father of her child regardless of any blood test results. After our son Austin was born, I took the DNA swab test at her request and we found out Austin was not mine. None of this changed or altered my feelings for her or Austin. Not once did I ever look at him or even think of him as not being my son. Till this very day those feelings for him have never swayed. After Austin was about two years old, Heather broke down and told me she was in fact never raped. She simply had a fling with some guy and didn't want to tell me. This information two years after he was born hurt me in ways I could never put in words. She deceived me in the worst possible way and robbed me of the choice to give up my childhood or not. I cannot say for certain if I'd have taken on the responsibility of fatherhood had I known the truth from the start. I do know that I have no regrets of being there for my son. He has been my heart, my pride and joy, since the moment I knew he was due to be born. Heather swore to me that no matter what happened between her and I, Austin would know no other father than me, and she would never keep him from me. Years later, after I was released from my prison term, Heather started acting different with me. She rarely would let me spend time with Austin. Didn't like me taking him to my mom's home. When I moved from my mom's, she didn't let me take him to my house 'cause she said she didn't want him around my friends. What it boiled down to is we weren't together no more and she wanted to use our son as a pawn to try controlling me. The whole situation had me at a loss and made me want to stay wasted all the time so I could dull the pain I felt. After I committed my crime here in Florida, and was sentenced to death row, Heather continued to use Austin as a tool to inflict heartache upon me. I tried for several years to write Heather and Austin to be involved in his life as best as possible in the situation I'm in. She would write me a few times a year mostly only to speak ill of me and my family, and my girlfriend Andrea. She told me Andrea could never replace her and I was a fool to think otherwise. I continued to write her and explain I was only her friend and just wanted to be a part of our son's life. She didn't take that well. I couldn't get her to send me any photos of him even. Then she started only writing once each year on my birthday. I'd send Austin cards, drawings and letters never knowing if he was given any of the stuff. Then to my surprise she writes me saying she was in jail doing 60 days for a DUI and came to the realization that Austin needed me and missed me. He spoke of me often. My lil' man wanted his dad in his life and she claimed to be ready to allow that again. Told me she would start writing more often, send photos, and make sure Austin got anything I sent for him. I was so happy. Soon as Heather was out of jail I never heard from her again. I sent mail and it was returned to me saying no forward address.

"My grandpa writes me telling me Heather moved and said she wants nothing more to do with me or my family. Almost every weekend for many years my grandpa would pick Austin up and do stuff with him. Take him fishing, to parks, libraries and all the fun stuff grandpas do with their grandkids. For no reason what so ever she ended that and showed no concern for anyone else's feelings. Not only did she break my heart with her reckless actions, but she broke the hearts of my family. I can only imagine the pain she has caused our son by stopping him from contact with his family, my family, the only family he's known for his entire life. How can a woman be so cold hearted to her own child? He will be 13 years old this year.

"Another thing I wanted to share now, but didn't want to before is about Andrea. She is an amazing young woman that I met and started dating only three weeks before I was arrested on this capital murder case. She was only a year younger than me, age being 22. I always liked my women to be older than myself but with Andrea it didn't bother me because she was far more mature than her age. So beautiful, yet very insecure. A virgin who hadn't had any kind of real relationships. It was love and lust for us both immediately. For three weeks, we were rarely ever apart. I didn't want to hustle, go out with friends or do anything other than spend time with her.

"When I came to Florida it was Spring Break and there were females everywhere. That's something I'd normally take advantage of even while already dating someone. I was so stuck on Andrea that I didn't even notice a single female around me. All I wanted to do was talk to her on the phone and go back home to Wisconsin 'cause I missed her company. I couldn't even enjoy myself 'cause she was not with me. After being in Florida for about five hours or so, drinking and getting wasted, I got pulled over less than a mile from the bar I had left. For what reason, I don't know and never found out. I had a black dude with me named Deshawn Croton. After the cop came to my vehicle and took my ID back to his cruiser, I called Andrea and told her I needed her to come down to Florida right away to pick me up cause I got pulled over and was gonna pop the cop and ditch the truck. She said okay and I hung up.

"Deshawn Croton, heard this conversation and asked my intentions. I told him I was gonna smash off and pop at the cop. My intention was never to kill anyone. I meant only to pop off a few rounds at the cop to drive off. Hell, I was wasted and not thinking rationally. Before the cop made it back to my truck, Deshawn had jumped out and ran off into the crowd. When the cop came back to my truck he noticed Deshawn was gone. He then started pulling out his gun and reaching to try opening my door. I freaked out at the sight of his gun and immediately pulled my gun from under my thigh and started shooting at him as I hit the gas to get away. Next thing I know I'm back with Deshawn and had ditched the truck. I called Andrea again in front of him and asked if she was coming to get me. I told her what had happened and she said she was already on her way. Well, I already told the story of how I got arrested the next day.

"What I didn't tell yet is how Deshawn Croton snitched and told the police about Andrea. He told them I informed her of what I intended to do before I did it, then told her what I did afterwards and that she came down to come get me so I could leave the state. When the investigators first spoke to me wanting a confession, I wouldn't speak. Later they made threats to charge Andrea for conspiracy to aid a capitol murder fugitive across state lines. Without hesitation, I agreed to confess as long as they left her alone. I never expected Andrea to stick around and stand by me after I was arrested. I was surprised by her love, loyalty and commitment she showed me. I even told her on the phone that I didn't expect her to stick around. I told her I'd been locked up before while dating other women and was used to them abandoning me. She told me she wasn't like any other woman. She does what she says and she would be here for me until the very end.

"A few months later I was taken off my floor and put on lock down. Someone said I offered them $100,000 to help me escape – or so they say. Crazy shit 'cause it wasn't until this happened that I got any thought to try and escape. I got my hands on a cell phone another inmate had, and used it to call Andrea. I made plans with her to escape the jail, told her the risks she would be taking, the time she would be facing if she were caught, and she was still willing to help. Love makes people do crazy things. She came down to visit me and while here; yes, she managed to get me saw blades, a cell phone, cash money, drugs, and tobacco into the jail. As I said earlier, we were snitched on by a guy named Carlos Worlds who was an inmate at the jail. They never had any physical proof Andrea did anything. Of course, these days the government no longer sees physical proof as a requirement to charge and convict people of crimes. A simple accusation made by a convicted felon, who's trying to get a reduced sentence is good enough to charge and convict people these days. So Andrea was sentenced to three years in a FL prison. During those years we stayed in close contact by correspondence through our family. Our love continued to grow fonder. The relationship we have is simply amazing by any and all standards. We reached a level of communication, honesty, and trust that far exceeds even the highest of expectations.

"It's over six years later and Andrea is still here, not fading from my side even for a moment. We have fought to receive visitation for several years now without success. In fact, the only reason I decided to share more about her, is because recently DOC told us she is permanently denied visitation. This news made us both see things in a new light. I can never again even see the woman I love. Death Row don't allow the use of phones, which means I'll never be able to even hear her voice again. I could never be so selfish to the woman I love and expect her to carry on a relationship under those conditions. She has been too good to me and deserves better. She has already sacrificed years of her life to be with me. Her love and devotion has never been in question. I don't think she will ever fully move on with her life until I'm gone. All I want for her is happiness. At this point in time I'm considering how best to go about helping her get it. I wanted to share with the world how wonderful and amazing my "sexy lady" Andrea really is. She has been down with me like no other and for that alone I couldn't be more grateful.

"The final thing I want to speak about is my case. Throughout the book, I mention things here and there. I didn't say too much because I'm going through the appeal process, and I know what I write will be used against me. At this point it matters none to me. I recently went to court on appeals for an evidentiary hearing. My defense team is trying to argue that I'm retarded. Reason being, I scored in the retarded range on the first IQ test I was given, and the state cannot execute a person found to be retarded. In no way am I retarded though. When I was given my first IQ test I was an ignorant 22 year old kid who had spent most his life locked up. I was fresh off the streets where my brain was fried from too much alcohol and drugs. I took the IQ test and did poorly. My lawyer then tells me I may be retarded. I was then required to take more tests.

The problem was my defense wouldn't pursue any other defense strategy other than this retarded issue. I was using my time wisely to educate myself, yet I was forced to try and to do bad on these tests in order to save my life. It's been over six years and I've spent mainly all that time educating myself on everything possible. I'm not that same dumb kid anymore. A retarded claim isn't going to work. What's sad is that I have legit claims that have been proven to the courts that should get me off death row, but these claims are said to not be reasonably established. *Substantially impaired capacity to appreciate the criminality of conduct and extreme emotional disturbance*, these are two of my claims my defense should have focused on. I also feel the court abused its discretion by ruling I failed to reasonably establish these claims. Their own State witnesses that testified against me testified to all the alcohol and drugs I had consumed. And as for the extreme emotional disturbance, I don't know many situations that could be considered more extreme than mine. It's a sad world we live in when the courts turn a blind eye to the law, sentence a man to death, and all because it was one of their own that was killed."

FALLEN ANGEL

Twenty-seven years before Angel Miles was sent to Death Row for the murder of a police officer, Manuel Valle ran a red light while driving a stolen Camaro. He was pulled over by Officer Louis Pena; Valle shot the officer and his partner. Valle was caught two days later and sent to Death Row. He fought off his fate for thirty-three years until the Governor signed the warrant for his death on June 30, 2011. He was executed on September 28 of that same year. It was 7:14 p.m. on a Wednesday, his third "date with death" and his last.

Oba Chandler had been sitting on Death Row in Union Correctional Facility for the better part of two decades since being convicted in 1994 for murdering a mother and daughters who were on vacation in Tampa, Florida from their dairy farm on rural Ohio. The bodies were found in Tamps Bay with concrete blocks attached to their raped, beaten and murdered bodies. He had raped them and then killed them in succession, each one being killed in front of the others. His death warrant was signed on November 11, 2011 and his final appeals were denied. He was taken out of his 6x9 cell to a 12x7 cell where he was put on Death Watch, sweating out his last moments on Earth. His last meal was modest: two salami and mustard sandwiches on white bread, one peanut butter and jelly sandwich on white bread and coffee.

Meanwhile, under the general strain of this looming execution, and the stench of Valle's death still palpable, Angel was slowly unraveling. The concrete walls could not insulate him from bad news and drama finding him:

"Got plenty of bad news today. Won't be writing for a minute. Grandpa had a serious stroke and is hospitalized. Wife had a car accident. Everything is just bad. I'm worried about my grandpa. Sucks 'cause he was gonna order me $100 dollars food package this month, but instead he's in the hospital. I don't want to think about that anymore. Um, next time you're on the computer, send a word to Heather and let her know about grandpa for me and that I'd love to get a letter from her."

Angel's mother, however, was tuned into the duress her son was under in his cell. She was, in fact, trying to move out of the past in order to reconstruct what is left of her life. She was done with blame and guilt:

"I didn't have a clue on things that he talked about. I as his mother feel somewhat ashamed not knowing of some of these things. It's been more than plenty to think about to know about stuff that he did or has been through, but I don't dwell on the past anymore like I used to because it took a real toll on my health, so I stopped blaming myself for my son being in prison. I can't take his place and I can't make him feel any comfort by telling him I was a bad mother. I can't change the past and I can't beat myself up over it. Just know this, I, like our God, have forgiven him for these bad things he has done in his life. I love my children like any mother. I don't ask why or what if any more; I just look after him. I am thankful for the people in his life right now, like you and some others that can see past what he is in prison for. Sometimes it is hard for people to look past that, to really see a person, the good in them, the kind of person they really are, not what they did and the bad choices they make in life doesn't tell what kind

of heart is in them or the deep feelings in them. I myself look at people and life so much differently than others. Well, anyway, I just wanted to let you know that I thank you for not judging my son and helping him. Thank you from my heart."

The public in general, however, would and did not forget what Angel had done. The Internet simmered with sheer animus and the worst of wishes for Miles:

Anybody who calls the murder of a police officer a "mistake" like you do, and claiming it is not a heinous crime, is out of touch with reality.

And repeating defense arguments already rejected by the jury and the appellate courts is not very convincing.

Don't worry; your scum-pal has another 10 years before he is executed.

Look he did it! No matter where he is from or what mental state he is/was in. Kill him now and be done with it. Stop supporting killers for the rest of the time I still pay taxes.

Save me a place in Heaven, brother.

I hope you burn in hell, punk. Don't bend over for the soap.

When you see worthless punks like this, doesn't it just make you want to put him in a room and beat the daylights out of him?

When someone has devalued life to the extent here, it's good to remember the Marines can always use Sniper targets!

I'd say take him to Camp Le Jeune [sic] and give him to the folks who can help straighten things out for him!

Then, as summer ended and cooler weather crept over Starke, Florida, Miles finally came undone. At night the temperatures hovered above freezing and the heating system of the prison failed: Hell froze over. The guards clamped down due to the impending execution of Oba Chandler. Cells were tossed; contraband was found in Miles' cell; he got a disciplinary write up. He was taken to a deeper, darker circle of this Hell, "the hole," where he literally was stripped of everything and left to freeze, starve and heal the wounds he got from a "disciplinary" beating. Another inmate familiar with Angel related what happened:

"Poor Miles is downstairs under me in a pair of boxers on a strip cell, DC, the hole, for three days. I'm like Duh!, you picked a fine time to snap and do that crap, "UGH"! I'm not sure what the whole story is but he asked me for your address and he'll probably write to explain, in the mean time, he needs our help so I'll tell you what I know.

Last Saturday, a week ago, he got put on DC (disciplinary confinement) for contraband – 15 days. Well I guess he declared a "psych-emergency" for some reason. So they took him to the Bug-Hut (psych. Building) and beat him up for no reason. Hmmmm? Then, didn't feed him for 2 days, I guess they thought he was faking it to get out of his DR, to get off DC.

Anyhow, that's not procedure, so he wants people to file a complaint with the Florida Department of Corrections if you can or will.

Yesterday, Friday, they put him downstairs again in cell 4106 I think (in a pair of boxer shorts) so if I'm cold, he has to be freezing, this is not procedure – cruel and unusual punishment, no heat, etc. (Even if he did something to deserve it). No mattress, no sheets, no toilet paper, etc. I guess it's the new way to try to get us to snap? Who knows what they are up to? But it is crazy, but we are pretty sure that Tallahassee is not aware of it, so he wants us to file complaints for him, since he can't do it – e-mail? Whatever? If you can or will.

I'm not sure what we could do to help, declaring a psych emergency was pretty dumb. They don't do anything to help you at all even if you need help, o it only makes it worse.

Maybe he is trying to get stronger meds out of the doctor, who knows? But, I guess they make sure you don't want to do it again unless you really, really need it, (a psych. emergency). Because they don't have time for B.S. and if you want/need attention, they will give it to you, (like most Big Brothers would), "UGH"!

I'm not sure how bad it was, but sometimes the nurses will tell on the guards if it was too bad, so? They are all scared of getting fired too, so I doubt they did much damage.

Anyhow, the more it happens, the more it will get reported, then hopefully all of it will stop soon, or sooner. (I hope.)

For now all I can do is write these letters and pray and try to stay out of it myself, off DC, etc. Hopefully all of the crap will blow over."

Word travelled back to Angel's family about his episode. His younger brother, James, was shocked and concerned that this incident would negate any progress he made during his last court date:

"That is the first I have heard, and thanks for keepin' me up to date. What the fuck is he thinkin'? That's going to fuck him up more. We did so much for him at the trial and shit. OMFG [oh my fucking God] I guess he is giving up on his fuckin' life and sayin' fuck it all. And that makes me want to cry, but thanks and, yes, please do keep me up to date and let me know what I can do to help if anything."

Heather, who knew Angel as well as anyone, at least as intimately as anyone, was more cynical if not realistic about Angel and his situation:

"That's Angel for u!!

"He gave up a long time ago. And just showing you are there is enough. What would you do if you were incarcerated on your life.... miss ya B!!"

No matter what anyone, close or distant, though, the Angel had fallen – to the deepest and darkest pit of that Hell they call a *correctional institution.* He has nothing but his boxers. No light can penetrate that darkness that surrounds him. The life he tried to steal and hold – all the women, all the money and all the booze and drugs – moved closer to one of those 12x7 cells that Oba Chandler munched on his salami sandwiches and sipped his coffee and Manuela Valle waited out the final three-hour stay of execution.

Angel is waiting for death, but then again, every human is waiting for death. It is only a matter of when, where, why and how – all the details. The quality of the life that is lived makes the difference between tears of remorse, sobbing in shame or keening with joy. In the Angel's case, Shakespeare may have said it best. To paraphrase the Immortal Bard: there was some sound; there was plenty of fury; there was a play and the curtains were drawn. But what remained? Did it mean anything at all?

No one will ever really know. What we do know is that in the end, the Angel will be strapped down to a board and the needles will press their steely tips through his skin, into his veins and then pour their poisons into his system. He will weaken; he will fade into a sleepy void; then his lungs will stop and so will his heart. But the questions linger: What did this Angel's life signify? Was it a victory for Order over Chaos? Was it Law over the Renegade? Is this civilization? Are we still human? Or, was it just blood for blood, an eye for an eye and a tooth for a tooth? Ultimately, it is a matter of perspective.

A few things are for sure. He will die at the hands of a private citizen who is paid to perform the execution; he will be over eleven-hundred miles from Milwaukee where the whole story of the Angel began. Whatever is still left in his cell will be claimed by his family, packed up and mailed from Florida back home. If his family does not have the money to bring his lifeless body home, then he will be buried in a field not far from the prison in which he spent the last of his days. A hole will be dug and he will be lowered down into it. Dirt will be thrown on him. The only vestige of Michael "Angel" Miles, Jr. will be a metal license plate in an open field that states his name, date of death and inmate number:

Michael Miles, Jr.
DOD: xx/xx/20xx
128135

May you rest well in death, Angel, like you never could in this life. Rest in peace.

[1] "hood" is slang for "neighborhood."

[2] "tripping" is slang for getting angry or out of control.

[3] "feeling" something or someone is slang for having a deep connection

[4] "slinging" means selling

[5] A "plug" is a connection for obtaining stolen merchandise in some way from a store; a "blunt" is a hollowed out cigar into which marijuana is placed and then smoked.

[6] "yellow" indicates one of mixed African and Caucasian descent

[7] Large quantities

[8] "tip" is slang for point of interest

[9] "smoking out" is smoking a great deal of marijuana over a long period of time

[10] This is slang for being as mad or "hot" as a recently fired .38 caliber pistol.

[11] "trying" someone is slang for attempting to dupe someone in some way.

[12] "fire" means very intense in some way.

[13] A "contact high" is indirect intoxication from second-hand smoke of marijuana.

[14] Slippers used in the shower

[15] "swag", in this case, is short for "swagger" or attitude.

[16] "Mugging" is staring at someone menacingly or suspiciously.

[17] A "stack" is a thousand dollars. A "5 stack" is five thousand dollars.

[18] To "do me" is to care of yourself above all other considerations.

[19] Law Enforcement Officer

AFTERWORD

Angel Miles' sentence of death was commuted to Life after the Florida Supreme Court deemed it necessary for a unanimous vote (12-0) in favor of the death sentence. Miles' jury originally came back 11-1. Though confined, Miles will live.